From Behind the Badge to Behind Bars

LONNIE MARSHALL

AuthorHouse™
1663 Liberty Drive
Bloomington, IN 47403
www.authorhouse.com
Phone: 833-262-8899

Because of the dynamic nature of the Internet, any web addresses or links contained in this book may have changed
since publication and may no longer be valid. The views expressed in this work are solely those of the author and do not
necessarily reflect the views of the publisher, and the publisher hereby disclaims any responsibility for them.

Any people depicted in stock imagery provided by Getty Images are models,
and such images are being used for illustrative purposes only.
Certain stock imagery © Getty Images.

This book is printed on acid-free paper.

ISBN: 979-8-8230-2438-9 (sc)
979-8-8230-2439-6 (e)

Library of Congress Control Number: 2024906337

Print information available on the last page.

Published by AuthorHouse 04/10/2024

authorHOUSE®

This book is dedicated with love and respect

To God all mighty, My Mother Kay, My Soul mate

And to all my peers,

Who never stopped inspiring me?

In loving memory of

Kay Frances, Woodham, Marshall, Hix

Mama & Papa Winters

Mama & Doc Segrest

Mama & Roy Kadenhead

Table of Contents

AUTHORS BACKGROUND

Introduction

On July 16, 1964, in a small-town hospital, in DeFuniak Springs, Florida, a baby boy was born to Kay and L.O. Marshall. They named him Lonnie, he had two stepbrothers from his father's first marriage and two sisters with his mother Kay.

This is based on his life from birth to date as he lived. This is a true story. You will hear how he was raised, abused (physically, mentally and sexually), how he trained animals, followed his goal to be a Law Enforcement Officer, came out as a gay man, got accused of murder, went to prison for robbery, released on parole, how he had 1053 sex partners, how his goals changed, Owns his own business, found the one he loves and will hopefully marry, received a pardon and where he is in life today.

He will try to use only people's first names so no one will know who they really are or be offended. But some of the officers last names' because that is the only thing, I know them by.

Writing this book will bring back memories that he has blacked out of his life. So, watch out reading this story because it could carry you on a ride, he doesn't ever want to take himself.

This book is not written for teen age readers due to the language. Some of my friends will probably part company once they read this book. But I'm the same guy they were friends with before they read my hidden secrets. OH WELL!!

Books

From Behind The Badge To Behind Bars -

Birth to 31

This is based on his life from birth to date as he lived, this is a true story. You will hear how he was raised, abused (physically, mentally and sexually), how he trained animals, followed the goal to be a Law Enforcement Officer, came out as a gay man, got accused of murder, went to prison for robbery, released on parole, and met the devil in a relationship.

I Thought I Found Love, Back To Prison -

31 to 38

I meet the devil not the person I thought I was in love with, and then was sent back to prison because I was not going to live with a demon.

Living Around Millionaires And Back To Prison -

38 to 51

Met a millionaire in prison and lived around millionaires after I was released from prison, and back to prison once again.

Living Like A Millionaire And Finding My Soul mate -

51 to 59

Got out of prison, lived like a millionaire, received a Pardon from the Alabama prison system, found my soul mate but I have to wait for him to get out of prison to marry and live our life.

***** TO BE CONTINUED*****

Acknowledgements

For their encouragement, belief, had compassion, polished the expressions, within my mind, for sharing my vision. The author wishes to thank: God all mighty; my Mother. Dave my pastor and Shepherd, Wylene with her magical inspiration, Gary wisdom and grace, Richard for commitment and loyalty as a soul mate, Mrs. Segrest & Mrs. Swearington for their leadership and teaching. Charlotte for being the sister I never had, and Margaret for being my Mother hen and friend. Thank you each for the efforts, time, love, sacrifice, and making me a better man.

Special Thanks

Richard Horton for drawing the book's cover,

Named Stern Fallen.

It's a German word for Fallen Star.

CHAPTER 1

1964

Lonnie was raised in a small town of Bonifay, Florida on a 180-acre farm where they had horses, cows, pigs, a goat, chickens, and dogs. Bonifay was so small they didn't have a hospital at the time, so his mother had to be taken to Defuniak Springs to a hospital so he could be born.

Lonnie's mother was a housewife that took care of the house, farm, and kids. Lonnie's father was a pipe fitter and welder that traveled a lot, building paper mills, (Pine Bluff Arkansas, Panama City Florida, Some place in Ohio and Texas. Plus abused his wife and kids.)

Let me introduce you to my family, my two brothers from my father's first marriage, Steve and Lonnie (which we called Keith his middle name), my two sisters, Ramona and Pat. We were all born three years apart. I would have a set of twins as siblings, but my father kicked my mother with a pair of steal toe boots and caused Mother to lose them. I was the baby of the bunch. My grandmother Marshall, which was my father's mother lived on the farm, my grandfather Marshall, died before I was born. My grandmother Marshall had 13 kids.

Then on my mother's side of the family, Big Granny my mother's Grandma (Mrs. Donaldson) and my mother's mother Big Mama (Mrs. Felder), who had 9 kids. My mother's father died after World War I, I never met my Grandfather's. So, I made up my own families which you will hear more about Mama & Papa Winters, Mama & Doc Segrest, and Mama & Daddy Kadenhead.

My first memories of life are of my animals and school. But I do have pictures of me around a year old in diapers riding horses. Then around 3 years old setting on a deer, with a shotgun. Also, me setting in a watermelon that was so big I could stretch my legs out in.

Me & my first deer

1965

Mother use to tell me the story of when I was a year old and my sister's Pat and Ramona were bathing me. They put me in the tub and were bathing me. The water got cloudy from the soap and one of the girls dropped the soap into the tub. They started filling around in the tub trying to find the soap and come up with a piece of dodo in their hand where I had crapped in the tub. It was hard to get the girls to bath me from that day forward. I started off young in life a mean little turd. LOL!

When I was learning to talk mother saw me staring out into the yard through the door. And she asks me what was I watching? I said, "I'm looking at the man up in the tree." She walked to the door and looked and said, there's no one out there in a tree. I said, "Oh yes there is, he's setting up there in that big limb." She said, ok describe him to me. I told her what he looked like, and I thought she was going to fant. I had described my grandfather to a tee. My grandfather had died before I was born. So I guess he had come back and checked in to see me and let me see him.

1967

We had dogs we used to hunt deer with, Boy did we, and at one time we had at least 14 hunting dogs. At the age of three I would watch T.V. where they would hook dogs to snow sleds. Well, I had the dogs, whip, red wagon, no snow, but miles of dirt roads and fields. I would hook at least 6 dogs to my red wagon at a time, walk them out on the dirt road jump into my red wagon and crack my whip and down the road we would fly. The steering was not that good, and the stops were even worse. Those dogs knew that I could draw a blister on their butts with that whip. So, they knew to run when I cracked that whip. The problem was they did not know what Gee and Haw meant, and even worse know how to stop or what Woo meant. So, I just had to hold on and ride it out until they stopped on their own or I jumped off the back of the wagon and drag my feet holding on to the wagon until they stopped. Boy it could be a wild ride some days. I just could not get caught doing this by my father or he would use my whip on me for whipping his dogs.

Our father was so mean; I use to have to cut the lawn at the age of three. With him being a welder, he made the push mower so I could push it to cut the yard. Plus working on the farm, we had our chores. My chores were mowing the yard when the grass needed cut, feed horses, pigs, chickens, and the dogs. Plus, if we had calves that had to be bottle fed, mother and I would bottle feed them. If it was not done when father came in from being on the road working, she and I would get beat.

Just to let you understand before we get to deep into my life my father never told us he loved us, but our mother would tell us most every day. Father thought that love was giving you a roof over your head and food in your stomach.

1968

Back in 1944 I think, Bonifay started the first Rodeo,(the rodeo is always held the first week in October) I can remember every year of my life either being at the rodeo watching or riding horses in the parade and grand entry. I was too little at the time to participate in the rodeo. But in time I would be helping do everything. I stayed be hide the bucking shoots learning how to do everything. I wanted to be a rodeo bull fighter. But just a little too small at the time.

I think that this was the same year father got drunk when we were getting ready for the rodeo. Mother made us take all the horses to town and hide the cars and trucks that no one was driving, so father would not have anything to get to town on. Well we took and hid all the vehicles, but a hunting car, the old Henry J car. Father took the back seat out caught Ring-O our Shetland pony rolled the windows down and made Ring-O get in and stick his head out the window. He drove to the rodeo drunk as hell. We did not know he was anywhere on the rodeo grounds. My brother Steve looked at the horses in the grand entry and saw someone who looked like a clown on a small horse fall off in a crowd of over 600 horses. Steve looked around and saw me even though I was four I could ride a horse like you never knew, I was talking to the rodeo clown (Mr. Dobbs) setting on my horse. It was our father drunk riding Ring-O with Vote for George Wallace stickers stuck all over the horse. We were all so embarrassed, hoping he would be stomped to death by all the horses. But to surprise, he come out with only one horse stepping on him. God takes care of fools and drunks. I was hoping people didn't know that drunk was our father.

This is one of those things that you try to black out of your head as a kid. But it sticks in your head for ever at the age of four.

My two oldest brother's lived most of the time in Panama City Florida with their mother Maxine. We had a house down there that we would stay in on some weekends. We had a contract to furnish the Petticoat Junction Amusement Park and Ghost town. I think it opened in 1964 when I was born and we would switch out horses every two weeks with fresh horses for the Ghost town gun fights until it closed in 1984.

Father loved to go Deep Sea fishing, I went with him one day and back then the roads in Panama City were really narrow and had deep ditches on each side of the roads. Well the traffic was backed up because a black man was walking on the road so the traffic couldn't get by. Understand us kids were taught to drive at a very young age, even though we couldn't touch the peddles we would use sticks to touch the gas and brakes and I would stand up in the seat to look over the dash of the car. So father got mad and told me to get under the wheel while he jumped into the back seat. He rolled the back window down and took one of his deep sea rods out the window. I used a small poll to mash the gas, he told me to keep going when we got to where the black man was walking down the road. The other cars were going around him when the other line was clear, but I was told not to. Father took the rod and hit him so hard it knocked him down into the ditch, and we kept on going. Bet that guy never walked on the road so cars couldn't go by anymore.

1969

At the age of five I helped raise two calves. A white steer Charolais calf, I named him Bully and a white face heifer we named Girly. My mother had to teach Girly how to suck the bottle, but Bully would knock me down to get his bottle. We put collars on both and tied them together with a rope. So, when they were out in the field, they were easy to catch. Because Bully was tame and would come when it was feeding time, we would call Bully and he would drag her with him. As time went a long Girly became tame as well. But we kept them tied together. I started playing with Bully training him to kneel and let me sit on his back. Later I would ride him around in the field. They grow to be nice looking calves.

I had started going to Head start, so I was working on the farm plus school. When the calves grow up to about 650lbs. or 800lbs. somehow, they run away. But about two weeks later, our freezer was full of beef. I never figured out why my calves run away, until I got old enough and figured where they went, then my mother told me. She said, your father killed them for meat.

That made me hook his dogs up to the red wagon and fire their asses up with my whip. I could not get back at him, but I could fire up his favorite dogs. He would wonder why they were hard to catch sometimes. I think he figured it out when he found whip strips on a few of them. Well they didn't want to mind me; father would whip me for not minding, so I thought that's how you teach them to do right by beating. Plus, it let me treat them like I wanted to do him.

As time went on, I trained the dog team to take me to granny Marshall's house. She lived 40 acres away. That's a nice ride with 6 dogs pulling a red wagon. Granny's house was about 3 feet off the ground, (picture this) me in a red wagon going down a dirt road as fast as 6 dogs could run with NO brakes or way to tell them to turn left or right. When we got to Granny's yard, they would take a turn right up into her yard and head toward her house that is about 100 yards off the dirt road. We would go under the front porch of the house and I would grab the bottom of the porch with my hands while sitting in the wagon, now try to stop 6 run away dogs, they can snatch the wagon out from under you, just saying from some experience.

Now about head start school experience? I would do well in class until I would see one of my sister's walk by the classroom. I would want to go be with them. My teachers would catch Hell trying to keep me in class. If they would ever touch me, I would turn into a mad dog. I would grab them by the leg, arm, or whatever I could get a hold of and bit them. The school we were in held head start through 6 grades. If I remember right it was an old three-story brick building. The classrooms were on the wall sides and the gym was in the center of the building. So, if you were on the third floor you could look down on the gym through the wooden guard rails. I went there for head start and Kindergarten.

1971

In my first-grade class they had built a new Elementary School. Holmes County Elementary it had outside basketball courts and my favorite place was the playground monkey bars, see saws, and the Map of the United States that was painted with all different colors. Our first bus driver that I remember was Mr. Williams. There's a lot to say about Mr. Williams later in this book. Guess what he turns out to be?

Back to the farm. I told you we lived on a 180 Acre farm our closest neighbor was at the end of our property a half mile away. That was the Byre Family, 3 boys and 1 girl, Mike, Tim, Rendell and Regina. Their father was in prison for making Moonshine, but when he got out he owned his own logging company.

1973

When I was nine years old, I had tonsillitis. My fever went up to 106.3 and would not go down. My mother had started to work as a nurse/supply clerk at the New Holmes county Hospital. So, they put me in the hospital and packed me in ice to get the fever down. After three days in the hospital my father came into my room and told me I was taking up someone place that was sick bed, get my close on he was checking me out. Well I got dressed and we left the hospital. He took me to a little restaurant on the edge of town, Mr. Brown's restaurant. When we walked into the restaurant Mr. Brown came over, he noticed I was sick and asks me what was wrong. I told him I was sick; my tonsils were swollen up I had a fever. He said, I'll be right back. Mr. Brown's place was known for the best ice cream in town. He came back with an ice cream cone at least a foot tall. He told me to eat that, it was good for what ail me. I eat the whole thing; we went home, and I went to bed. The next morning, I got up I had NO fever and my tonsils had went down. I was healed. Come to find out Mr. Brown had mixed moonshine into my ice cream. I have not been sick with a fever since that day.

A lot happened while I was 9 years old. I received my own dog that I picked out from Mr. Bynum who owned and raised large Brahman Bulls on his ranch about 3 miles from our house. He had white English/pit mixed bull dogs to work cattle. I sat in the room where the puppies were and I guess he picked me as well as I picked him, my little boy who I named Pumpkin. I took him home at 8 weeks old, we lay in the floor and watched T.V., when it was time to go to bed, and I took him to bed with me. My Mother said, no that's not going to work. But I begged her to let him sleep with me because he was a baby and needed me to be with him. Well she let him stay. Pumpkin and I went hard and fast to sleep. He slept on the pillow next to my head. The next morning mother came in my room and woke me up. She said, the dog has got to go outside. I ask her why he's been asleep on the pillow by me all night. She said look on the foot of the bed. Oops! Sometime during the night Pumpkin got up and pooped on the foot of the bed. I know that would be the last night he got to sleep in the house especially with me we lay there and looked at each other; he didn't know he had done anything wrong he was only a baby. From that night on he slept outside beside the front door on the car port. We were the best of friends and everywhere I went he went. He grows up to be a 120lb. dog. How do I know he got that big? I trained him to get on the bathroom scales to be weighed.

I'm in the third-grade year in school; my father had quit traveling welding and bought a welding shop in Bonifay. The building was so big my mother opened a restaurant/oyster bar, pool hall on one end. Next to the restaurant we had a small parts store, next to that was the small engine repair shop, next to that we had a welding shop. Then we rented out the other part of the building to an auto body shop.

Understand, we still had the farm that we kids had to keep running. I was 9 years old mowing the fields with a tractor and bush hog. I'm not tall enough to reach the brakes and clutch on an old Allis-Chalmer tractor with no power steering. Also plow and plant the fields with corn, plus keep the family garden.

The neighbors that lived to our west were the Fish Family. They went into the real-estate business and bought a larger house closer to town. They rented out their house to Mr. & Mrs. Al Winters from Canada. They retired and came down to buy land and build a home. But, until then they rented the Fish house, which was a very nice four-bedroom house on 60 acres with a peach orchard.

My father came up with this great idea, even though we had the farm and shop to take care of, why not lease the neighbors peach orchard out and let the public pick their own peaches and pay for them and let us kids pick peaches so we could sale them at the shop, grocery stores on town and let Lonnie take the truck with the camper and setup a road side market in front of Simbo's Truck Stop. Even though I was 9 years old and the girls were 12, and 15, I got to sale peaches. While I was out selling peaches Papa & Mama Winters would come by and check on me. They thought it was odd for a young boy not to be able to run and play like other kids, but to be working at my age.

We picked peaches, sold peaches, and made peach brandy out of the peaches that were going bad. Did I mention we still had to feed all the animals and keep up the farm? This was in the summer of 1973 while we were out of school and didn't have a lot to do.

Mama Winter's had a sister that came down from Canada to live with her, her name was Aunt Hank. Those two would get in the kitchen and cook fresh breads, cakes, and cookies. One of my fondest memories of them was one day they made a batch of lemon cookies and gave me some. Pumpkin was about 6 to 8 months old by then, he had very good manners. Aunt Hank gave him a cookie at the sliding glass door. He took it very nicely from her, then took it over to a tree dug a hole and buried it, she thought that was the funniest thing, she then knew that batch of cookies were bad. But Pumpkin was so sweet how he took the cookie and not just dropping it in the yard but went behind a tree and buried it.

They told the story of one kid that came over to their house in Canada. Their property adjoined the zoo property. She said, the kid came running into the house and said there was a Gorillaophant in the back yard. Which it was an Elephant. The way they described the kid coming into the house saying there was a Gorillaophant made it so funny.

Since it was the summer and we were out of school I would go and ride my horse and check the fences. I would have to ride in front of our neighbor's house the Byre's. Well one day when I was out riding Tim came out and spoke to me in the woods. Well we as young boys explored into the sexual parts of life. That's when I realized I enjoyed having sex with a man more so than woman.

Tim's brother Rendell and I were the same age and in classes at school. If I were to have had a school puppy love it would have been Lynn. She had long beautiful hair. Plus, her daddy owned the I.G.A. Grocery in Bonifay.

We had a small pond close to our house where some of the animals got water and we had stocked with fish. My granny Marshall and I would go down and fish sometimes. One day while fishing we saw a gator about 4 feet long. I went and got one of father's deep sea rods and through the line over the gator back. I started reeling it in; when I got to the gator I snatched the hook and caught the gator on the side. As I started reeling it in granny ask what I was going to do with him. So, I let her hold the pole while I went to get a wire cage that we had. I took the gator and put it in the cage. I had granny to call the Florida Game and Fish Commission to come get it and relocate.

I don't remember very much about my 1st, 2nd, and 3rd grade of school other than being the favorite kid of the bus driver. Mr. Williams would always let me run the bus lights or open and close the door on the bus until I got off the bus. Every now and then I got to steer the bus while he got on to the other kids for acting up.

1974

As we start back to school in 1974, I took my place back running the bus lights and opening the door. I joined the school choirs I sang very high tenor. If I remember right Mrs. Treadwell was our music teacher.

My mother was very religious lady took us kids to church most every Sunday. We were members of the Gully Springs Baptist Church. My mother sang in the quire. We started our own family Gospel singing group. My oldest sister played the piano and we would sing. I can remember one of everyone's favorite songs we sang because I sang it so high, Jesus is coming soon. If I had a dollar for every time, we sang that I would have been a millionaire at an early age.

That same year I started my piano classes. Every afternoon the bus would drop me off at my piano teacher's house. She was also the piano player for the church we went to. That didn't last long, because father wanted me home to work on the farm. Too many things had to be done and not playing a piano was one of them.

Our town also hosted the Biggest All-Night Gospel sing in the world. As Uncle Harvey use to say every morning on his WBGC radio show. This is your good old friend Harvey Etheredge coming to you from the WBGC radio station in Bonifay, The home of the Bonifay Blue Devils, the Championship Rodeo, the Biggest all night singing in the world and a lot of good people and that's you I'm speaking of. You hear that every day for 10 years and you'll remember it to. That's how he would start his show. I even got to be on his show several times.

Every year the weekend that was closest to July 4th we had the Biggest All Night Gospel Singing in the World. The singing would start when the sun went down and would stop when the sun come up. This singing would bring in all the best gospel singers like, The Happy Goodman Family, Florida Boys, Dixie Echoes, Cloud Indian Family, Chuck Wagon Gang, LeFevre Quartet, Louis Family, Spears Family, plus many others. We carried our lawn chairs, blankets, and ice chest. You better carry your rain gear also because in July we would have pop up rain showers. Later in years I learned if I took a roll of plastic I would make money selling plastic to people that didn't know anything about the Florida weather.

Since I brought up the Rodeo let me talk about that for a minute. The Long Family and Reynolds Family started the Rodeo back in 1944 and our family has always played a part in it. It has always been held the first week of October. Our family has always ridden in the parades and Rodeo's. That was always my high life of the year. I have never missed a Rodeo when able to go. I loved everything from working the livestock, the animals be bucked, trick riding, and comedy shows with the clowns. As I grow older you will hear some stories of me being the barrel clown.

I told you we had pigs, but I did not say how many. We had over 300 breeding sows and three boars and God knows how many pigs at any time. New pigs every 3 months, 3 weeks and 3 days hogs have pigs.

We would have sometimes 600 feeder pigs and all the young boars had to be cut. That means we would have to cut their nuts out so they would grow faster and not have a bad taste when you kill them. On nut cutting day people would come from miles to get young mountain oysters to take home and fry an eat.

People could not believe that I was 10 years old and all the things I could do especially shot a rifle. I started to learn how to shoot a gun around the age of 4 or 5. We would take a .22 rifle and kill rats. We had a feed house where we kept all the pig food, horse food, dog food and some cow food. It had a concrete floor and the rats would tunnel under it. The rats would also tunnel under the dog pen and faring pen. Father would not let us shoot the ones under the dog pen and faring pen, because we could miss and kill an animal, but the one's under the feed house were fair game. If they stuck their head out of the hole, we would kill them. I got so good at shooting I could strike kitchen matches on the fence post. As for the rats under the dog pen and faring pen we would gas or fish for them. You're probably scratching your head wondering how do you fish for a rat. Well you take a fishing rod and reel put a treble hook on the line put food on the hook set it in front of the rat hole spool off about 30 yards of line get a chair and set. When the rats comes and grabs the food let him run back in the hole and start eating the hook and try to pull him out of the hole. Now when you get the rat worked out of the hole you can wait until he gets in the open and shot a moving target or fight him on the rod until he tires down. Because when he first comes out of the hole, he will go wild, jumping 3 to 4 foot and running everywhere. Don't let him run under something because it's a fight to get him out again. Keep the line as tight as you can.

Now you see how we passed time when not busy working. It was with rat fishing or Rattlesnake hunting. Yes, Rattlesnake hunting. We use to go on our property and international paper property that a joined our property and check gopher holes for snakes. We would catch all kinds of snakes, Rattlers, Black, green, Oak, Rat, Spitting Attars, Cotton mouth, King, Copperhead, and coil. We were lucky and never got bit by a poison one because we used sticks with loops to handle them. If they were not poison's we would have blood all over our hand from them biting.

We would go to Panama City, Florida and take the snakes to the Reptile World, they would pay us $2 or $3 dollars a snake and $10 a foot for rattle snakes. That's how we made our extra spending money. We would also catch rattle snakes and take them to the Opp, Alabama Rattlesnake Rodeo. People would bring snakes from near and far to put them in the rattlesnake pit so they could watch the snake show and see them racing snakes and milking snakes. Then we would kill some and eat them, they would use the snake hides to make wallets, belts, hat bands, and vest.

One day I told mother we were going to catch snakes. Well my mother is very scared of snakes; she would hurt you. Anyway, we went out and did not catch any snakes, so I took a burlap sack and put jumper cables in it, and they would bounce around in the bag like something was alive moving in it. I took the bag into the house and mother was in the kitchen where I went to show her what I had caught. She knocked the sliding glass door off the track, she ran out of the house as fast. I got a spanking that day.

One night while we were asleep, I heard father fighting with mother. My sister's and I got up and saw what was happening. Father had the fire poker beating mother with it, he knocked her into the gas heater, and she was getting burnt. My oldest sister got a butcher knife, Pat got a frying pan and I got a shotgun. We stopped him from beating her and told him if he hit her one more time, we would kill him.

As a kid there are a lot of things you can't remember after getting old, if your abused, you black a lot of your life out to kill the pain you when through. Sometime between the age five and seven my mother separated from my father, we lived on the Pensacola Bay and my mother worked as a cook at Jerry's Seafood Restaurant & Bar. We only lived there through the summer. We didn't have to work on the farm anymore just play on the beach. There was a pier at the front of the house we used as a diving board swim day and night. One of my funny memories was Pat and a friend (Tracy) went skinny dipping in the Pensacola Bay, they left their close on the pier, I stole them and run into the house and locked the door, left them outside running around butt naked trying to get me to let them in.

Father begged mother to come back to the farm after the summer, so we went back to Bonifay, back to school, and back to work on the farm.

1975

We had a horse name Prince; he was part Clydesdale and Arabian a very big stub horse. We use to breed and make saddle bronco horses with big feet and bone. Anyway, mother and all of us kids could ride him, but if father tried to ride him, he would go crazy and throw him. Our father gets so mad if he can't ride a horse that we could. He said, "I'll ride him or kill him." So, he saddled Prince got on him and got throwed. He told me to catch the horse. He went to his truck and got a blackjack stick out; put it in the saddle horn. Now this time when he got into the saddle when Prince started acting up, he took the blackjack stick and started hitting him in the head. Prince started bucking and throwed his head into fathers head knocking him off busting his eye. When father got up, he was mad. He told me to catch him and take the saddle off of him and take him to the barn. So, I took the saddle off and went to the barn with him. While father went to the house to stop his head from bleeding. When he came out of the house, he told me to put Prince into the Bull head catcher. I lead him into the head catcher; father closed it on his neck. Prince fought so hard. When he started to calm down, father took out him pocketknife and cut Princes nuts off. At the same time Prince pulled his legs together making father cut his hand bad. Father said, "Turn him loose and put him into the barn." Prince was bleeding badly. Father told me to leave him alone, so I went to the house.

That poor horse bled all night. My Granny Marshall ask me the next morning, is that horse still alive. I said, "Yes, but still bleeding." Granny grabbed her Bible and told me to come to the barn with her. She said, "You should not treat a dumb brut like that." Prince was standing there too weak to move. Granny opened her Bible to Ezekiel, I'm not sure of the chapter. She slapped Prince on the hip and said, "Horse I don't know if you understand what I am saying, but I hope you believe it." She started reading from the Bible saying something about you should not waist in your own blood. I watched the blood go from a running stream to a drip, to stop. WOW!

A few weeks later, one night at home we were all setting watching T.V. father was sleeping in his recliner. A knock come to the door. It was one of the Deputies with the Holmes County Sheriff's Department; he asked father did we have a hound dog that would track humans. Father said, "No why?" The officer said he pulled a car over down the road from our house and the people got out and run into the woods. Father told him my boy has a Bull dog that will do anything he tells him to do though. So, father got his gun and told me to get on some close and get my dog. Pumpkin and I got into the back of the patrol car. When we got to where the people had run, the deputy showed me where the people had run into the woods. I told Pumpkin to go get them, we went through the woods and Pumpkin took us to where they were hiding under leaves and a log. That was my first time helping to catch someone.

While going to school I met a guy name Louis he had moved here from Brazil. He and his family moved here and were working on a dairy farm up in Esto, Florida just north of Bonifay. Louis told me that he had an Elephant, Wow I always wanted to have an Elephant and I wanted to see his. Well, I got on the school bus with him in the afternoon and went to his house to see the Elephant. When we got there he took me down to their big hay barn and we set there waiting on the elephant to come out of the woods. Well, it never happened, come to find out Louis had lied to me. But his mother and father said he did have one when they lived in Brazil. Here comes the bad part I had to call my mother and father and tell them where I was. It didn't turn out that bad I didn't even get a whipping for going to Louis's, they came and got me and took me home.

My mother's sister Mary Neil's kids would come down from Minnesota to visit, Connie would come stay with Ramona and Lisa would visit with Pat. We would always saddle up the horses and take them out riding. My cousin Lisa said she knows all about horses. I told her not to walk behind our red horse Flicka she kicked. She said, "She has been around horses before." Those Yankee's think they are so smart. I heard her scream. I ask what happened. Lisa said, "I think my leg is broken." The horse had kicked her. Well mother took her to the hospital and had a cast put on her leg. A few days later I ask her would she like to go help pick some peanuts so we could boil them. She wanted to know where the trees were, we pick the peanuts off. I told her peanuts had to be pulled out of the ground and picked off the vine. She thought all nuts grow on trees. I also got a laugh out of her telling my mother how good her biscuits were and wanted to know how she made them. Well mother told her she made them from scratch.

A few weeks later after my cousins had went back to Minnesota my mother got a phone call from Lisa, she said, "she had walked all over the store and could not find a box of scratch anywhere to make biscuits with." Boy how dumb are Yankee's?

Later that year father took us to Disney World in Orlando, Florida. Our first real vacation I knew of. We went with my mother's sister Norma and her family. I thought that was an amazing trip. My sister Pat and I road in the back of the truck in the camper. Most of the time we lay in the overhead bed looking at where we would be going. Once we got to Disney, we went to the Magic Kingdom. All those big draft horses pulling the trolley's, we even saw Mickey, Minnie, Goofy, Donald Duck, and the chipmunks. My favorite ride was, it's a small world, then the haunted house. They had to fight me to get on the 20,000 leagues under the sea. I was not going on that ride, but I got a whippen and still had to go on the ride crying. Then I went to see the Hill belly Bears, which made me feel lots better.

The next day we started back home. When we headed to Disney, we saw a lot of big horse ranches and orange groves. We saw signs saying, see the world's biggest Bull. Well on the way back home we stopped where the so-called biggest bull was at in this small zoo. The bull was not the biggest cow I had ever seen. But we still had fun.

When we got back home my cousins Ricky and Jim came to stay with us. We all had to sleep together and take showers together. I would hold them down in the tub and try to fuck them. They didn't like taking tub baths with me.

We had a rooster who would attack anything. The next day Ricky was outside playing on the tire swing, we heard him from inside the house screaming. I run outside to see what was going on and that rooster was spurring him while he was on the tire swing flying up and popping him with his spurs. I grabbed my whip and run him off.

That rooster was so mean he would try me some days. I caught him and took a saw and was cutting his spurs off. Mother told me not to do that because that was the only thing, he could defend himself with. The rooster got killed a few months later. He was chasing a car and got run over.

Later that year father took us to a Homelite and McCulloch chainsaw convention in Decatur, Alabama. We stayed in a big hotel that had a swimming pool. My sister's and I had to stay in our hotel room or at the pool; we could not go to the convention. My sisters would throw a beach ball out of the water and I would go got it. The tile around the pool got wet and I came out to get the ball, I slipped and knocked myself out. When I woke up there was a man with white hair, red jacket and white shirt standing over me saying, "Son are you ok speak to me son." I looked up and thought it was Santa Claus. But it was only Mr. Jerry Clower (the mouth of the south). He was there at the convention telling his stories of Marcel and the beer joint. That was my first time getting to see him. I had heard him on the grand ole Opry. My Uncle Charles that had a large plantation said I saw Mr. Clower when I was a small boy, but I don't remember that.

One of my father and Mother's friends owned the skating rink in Bonifay, it had a wooden floor. If I had a dime that I skated to the song (Rocking Robin) I would have been rich. Every Saturday night for as long as I can remember we would go skating on Saturday night and listen to the Grand ole Opry on the radio in the car. Every now and then on Friday night we would go to the drive-in movie theater. The only movie I can remember seeing was Grizzly Adams. I can also remember mother taking us to Chipley, Florida to an inside movie once called the Aristocats, it was a Disney movie.

In September we had a hurricane Eloise hit Florida and it knocked down the fences and some of our Bulls got out. Father told me to get on me horse and get them back in. I saddle my horse and went into the woods to bring the bulls out of the swamp and some of the bulls got after my horse and she had since enough to run and get away from them. On the way out of the swamp a vine get between my leg and the saddle, I pull my foot out of the stirrup and lay down on the saddle. When we got out of the swamp I stopped the horse and started back into the swamp after the bulls. It was still sprinkling rain and I felt something stinging my leg, I thought a bee was stinging me. I reached down and slapped my leg and my hand was full of blood. I looked down and my leg was bloody so I headed to the house. The vine was a wait-a-minute vine it has sticker 2 inches long, it had cut my leg to the bone. I went in the house and mother bandaged me up, and father told me to get my ass back out there and get those bulls back into the field. I still carry a scare on my right upper leg about 6 inches long.

The power was off for several weeks and we had a portable welding machine/generator. Father would go around to the neighbors and charge their refrigerators and freezers for $20 an hour so they would not lose their food. But every morning at 2am we would have to go the dairy farm and hook up the milking machines to milk cows and hand milk some of them. Then at 4pm we would have to do it again. Now you know how I got so much strength in my hands. This went on for several weeks until the power was back on.

1976

My sister who was 17 or 18 at the time started dating Terry. He sometimes would get drunk and mother would not allow him to drive home. She would make him come sleep in the room with me. I would wake up and he would be sucking my dick. I kind of enjoyed him getting drunk and staying over. I was having more sex with him than my sister was. He told me a few years later he and his next-door neighbor were lovers.

In the summer of 1976 Mother took us to my Aunt Mary Neil's in Minnesota and Aunt Joann (Woody) in Maryland. Boy what a long Greyhound bus ride. When we got to Minnesota, Aunt Mary and her girls took us to the country club to meet all their friends and let them make fun how country we talked. Well after about :45 minutes sitting there listening to them laugh at us, I turned the tables. A red dog had come in the side door and run under a table. I spoke up and said, "A big red dog just run up under that table." Lisa said, "Did you guys hear what he said, a Dawg just run under that table." I said, "No, I said a dog just run up under that table, not a dawg. Dog has not got an "A" in it. If you really want to hear something funny. Lisa thought peanuts grow on trees until I showed her how to pick them. Then she wanted to know if black people skin felt like ours, she had never seen one. She thought scratch, when you make biscuits come in a box. Now talk and laugh at me if you want, but that shit was really dumb and uneducated." You could have heard a pin drop there was no more laughing at the funny country boy and his family. When we got back to their house, I found out they were real people in their family. Their youngest sister Susan came riding up on her tricycle butt naked with her panties hanging on the handlebars. Now that girl is kin to me.

Their father uncle Kermit was a Minnesota Highway patrolman; he was one of my favorite uncles.

Well we left them and went to visit with Aunt Woody and her family. She had one girl Terri, and two boys Rusty and Randy. Her husband uncle Russ worked for NASA as an engineer. They had a very nice place. Rusty and Randy were close to my age. My mother said they caught me in the bathtub laying on one of them comparing peter size. I was not around them much after then.

After we made it back from Minnesota and Maryland for two weeks father was glad to have us to help him run the farm. He had just about had all he could handle between the horses, and pigs. I think the icing on the cake was Pumpkin would not help him work the cows, or pigs, and Sam my goat would not eat.

That same year while riding the bus to school, Mr. Williams told me to come back out and see him while he was parked out back waiting on the high school tutors and I did not think anything of it. Well while setting there talking to him, he squeezed my dick and said that sure felt good. I went back into the class and said something to some of the guys and they told the teacher. They fired Mr. Williams and hired Mrs. Ford as our new driver. I kept my set running the lights and opening the door.

We took another vacation Mother and father took me to Colorado to the Rocky Mountains. It is totally different than the Smoky Mountains. I did a lot of Mountain climbing that year. Mule deer everywhere. We also stopped in Kansas and saw some of the things that went on there. Some of the biggest livestock feed lots I had ever seen, thousands of cows.

Me & Sam my goat

Sam was a black goat that Cigar Smith the goat man of Bonifay gave me. The goat thought he was a dog; he would help Pumpkin work cows, and pigs. Some days Pumpkin and he would play chase. Sam would chase Pumpkin for a while then Pumpkin would chase him. When they get tried both would go dig a hole and lay down together.

I trained Sam to pull a buggy and do all kind of tricks, (Sit, Lay, Stand on a gallon can on all fours, push me in the swing, kneel down, bow down, and get into the truck.) I would ride him in some of the Rodeo parades and the Possum Day parade in Wawsaw.

1977

*W*ell. My sister Ramona got married to Terry and Billy the Bass singer for the Florida Boys gospel group was like our adopted father he came and sang at her wedding as a favor to Ramona.

Terry would get drunk and come to the house to talk to mother about his problems. She would not let him go home so he would have to stay and sleep with me, which was what he, was wanting. We would nut all over each other, and he loved it.

This year while at school in the 6th grade we would set in the center classroom on the floor and watch movies once a week. During the movie we would take our jackets and lay over our laps and the boys setting on each side of me Larry and Randy would jack me off. We never called ourselves gay we called it horsing around.

Father sold the big shop in Bonifay and had a welding and small engine shop built on our property across from the house. He bought me a magnetic sign making machine. I made signs for every business in Holmes and Washington Counties. That same year Mama & Papa Winters built their new house in Dogwood Lakes Country Club. Papa Winters loved playing golf. He took me once, but everyone on the golf course got mad because I wore my cowboy boots on the golf green. I could only drive the golf cart after that.

Terry

In the summer of 1977 Terry took me to South Florida to meet his Grandma, Aunts, and cousins. It was somewhere on the edge of Orlando. When we stayed at his cousins, Terry slept with his hot little cousin and I had to sleep on the couch. He told me he was fun in bed. I never got to find out, we stayed a week and come back. When we got back to Bonifay, Terry got a job out of town working in the Dothan area. So, we didn't get to see each other that much anymore. Ramona and Terry eventually moved up to the Dothan area.

The last week of summer father took mother and me to the Smokey Mountains. Pumpkin stayed home and took care of the farm. I think uncle Doy feed the animals. Since Sam would not eat the last time I was gone to Minnesota and Maryland we took him to stay with Cigar Smith where he could be with other goats.

We went to the Smoky Mountains and to Cherokee North Caroline. We saw Indians, bears, elk, deer, and chipmunks. We rode the mountain train and took the snow lefts to different mountains. Just to enjoy the time in nature.

When we returned home the farm animals were so glad to see me especially Pumpkin. The next day we went over to Cigars house to pick up Sam. When we arrived, Cigar said he was glad we were back, because that crazy goat would not eat and did not want to be around other goats. I told you he thought he was a dog. Cigar said, "Your goat went and got into the old chicken coop and would not drink or eat." If I would not have gotten back when we did, he would have probably starved to death. So, I walked into the field where the chicken coop was and started calling Sam. It was quite funny he started crying out yelling, he busted out of the chicken coop and came running to me, the hole time blatting like he was talking to me telling me all his problems, I told him to go get into the truck and lets go home. Pumpkin was waiting for him in the back of the truck. They were both happy again. When we got him home, he eat and drank until I thought he would bust, the whole time telling me and Pumpkin his problems.

Well it's October and rodeo time. This year at 13 years old I get to work as a barrel clown, I was taught by Mr. Dobbs a great rodeo clown, and one of the girls I was in school with Karen was going to be a trick rider on horseback. The rodeo was ready to start and the horses were lining up for the grand entry. I had my horse and goat to ride in the rodeo, Yee Haw! The rodeo was going well. Karen did well with her trick riding, and it was time for the bulls to start bucking. Time for me to roll out the barrel and set everything up to be the man in the can. The bulls started bucking and throwing cowboys everywhere, time for a joke. "Hey mister announcer call the vet; we have sick bull everywhere out here in the arena." The announcer ask how you know the bulls are sick. I said, "Because they are throwing up cowboys." About that time a bull hooked a guy and we got the bull off him. I run over to check on the guy and the announcer wanted to know if he was ok. I said. "Is blood brown?" The announcer said No, I said. "Then I guess he is ok then." I then told another joke. "Hey, I was down at the hotel in Bonifay today and saw a miracle happen today." The announcer said what was the miracle? I said. "there was a great big lady in one of those telephone booths and a little rat run across the parking lot and run up in the phone booth and up her leg, and she caught that poor little old rat with her knees." The announcer ask, "How was that a miracle?" I said. "I saw that woman squeeze over a gallon of water out of that poor little rat right there in that phone booth."

We bucked some good horses and bulls that night. The last bull they let out was one of Circle "D" rodeo ranch, meanest bull (Big Red). He was a clown killer, he hated clowns and barrels. That bull came out of the shoot straight to my barrel and throwed me and the barrel as high in the air as he could. We have handles to hold onto inside the barrel and some padding. So, it still hurts some. They ask me how I was; I told them "it felt like being dropped off of Niagara Falls in a barrel." After landing the bull came overlooked into the barrel to see where I was at and run his horn off into the barrel to see if he could get me. I went to the other end of the barrel so I would not get hooked. He rolled the barrel all around the arena until I got close to the fence and I crawled out and went under the fence out of the arena. The pick-up man got two ropes on the bull so they could control him, and drug him out of the arena.

That was our Friday night show. We still had Saturday night and Sunday shows to go. So, when it was all over, I was a tired young man. But no one got seriously hurt.

While in school this year our Chores teacher was Mrs. Berry, she took us to Troy College to compete in the southern singing division. We won the competition and would go to Nashville to compete. So later that year we loaded two buses with singers and a few adults to supervise and to Nashville we started. Almost half to way to Nashville the muffle fell off the bus we were riding in. Me and Mr. Berry crawled under the bus and fixed the bus with a close hanger, it was a hot muffler, but we got it hooked up and working again so it would not rumbled so badly.

Once we got to Nashville we checked into our hotel and got ready to go sing at the Grand Ole Opry. The next morning before the driver cranked the bus, I fixed the muffler better so it would not come off. We went to Opry Land and waited for our turn to sing. They gave us books with the entire Grand Ole Opry singer in it. I got all kind of signatures, Grandpa Jones, Roy Clark, Johnny Cash, June Cash, Roy Acuff, Cousin Aunt Minnie Pearl and several others. After we sang, we didn't win but we went on tours of the Opry stars and then rode the rides at Opry Land. Our trip back home was long but not as noisy as the trip up.

Later that year father said I was getting too big for my goat and buggy. If I didn't find someone to buy Sam, we would have him for our next goat dinner and make some good goat Brunswick stew.

I put a add on Uncle Harvey's radio station to sale Sam and he told people how well I had him trained. I got a phone call from a young guy and his mother. When they come to the house. I had a talk with him and Sam. The little boy was autistic, and I told Sam he had to be good and help the little boy, because he would give him a good home and take care of him, even though Pumpkin and I would not be there with him. I showed the little boy and his mother how to hook him to the buggy. After riding him around and showing him how to handle Sam. I showed them how he did tricks I had taught him. The mother and the little boy seemed like they loved Sam and would take care of him. I told them to come back with a truck and pick him up. They said No he can ride in the car, so we put the buggy in the trunk of the car and the goat in the back seat with the little boy, never to be seen again.

I was over at the welding shop and father told me to go cut the grass. So, I walked over to the house to get the push mower and saw bones in the yard and a water hose that needed put up. When I turned around father had his knife out cutting a switch out of a tree. I ask what are you doing? He said he was fixing to give me a whipping. I said why? Because I was not walking fast enough. I told him I had to roll up a water hose and pick up some bones so I would not run over them with the mower. He hit me across the back, and I run and picked up an axe. Mother came out screaming don't kill him he's your father. I dropped the axe and he hit me again. I run across the road where I had been throwing hay to the horses and got a pitchfork. When he got close to me, I stabbed him in the stomach. He dropped the switch and said I'll let you go this time. I said and I want kill you either.

1978

In January mother took me to Pensacola, Florida. She told father she would never come back if he did not change. Mother and I moved to an Appaloosa Ranch in Lillian, Alabama where we lived. I went to the 8th grade in Foley, Alabama. Father sold all the horses, cows, and pigs because he could not handle the farm and leased out the farmland.

The summer of 1978 we moved back in with father he said he had quit drinking, so mother gave in. I was happy to be back with my little buddy (Pumpkin). Father would not let me take him with me to Lillian, Alabama. Plus, a girl in Lillian gave me a young Palomino stud horse and I brought him back so I would have a horse. I named him J.R., because he was mean as J.R. Ueing on Dallas.

Since we did not have a lot going on at the farm other than a few hunting dogs, Pumpkin and J.R. the horse had a lot of free time. So, my school teacher Ma Sergest ask me would I like to help her clean her yard. They had 10 acres of flowers and flower garden. Her husband was still a doctor after 50 years.

She taught English and art classes at the Holmes County High School, I had to repeat the 8th grade. She had taught both of my sister's, and her husband was the oldest town doctor, he birthed my mother.

The rest of the summer I would help in their yard a couple a weeks and she would take me home. When school started back, she was my English and art class teacher. She treated me like her son. Everyone in Bonifay called me Sarah's boy, because when you saw one most of the time you would see the other or the other I was close by.

My father started working for the Holmes County Sheriff's Department. He was a jailor, dispatcher and deputy. On days I did not have to go to school I would go to the jail at night and help him dispatch, answer the phone, do NCIC and FCIC checks on cars and people, plus check on the prisoners.

One day on father's way to the Sheriff's Department, he saw the cows down in one of the swamps and heard dogs barking. The neighbor's dogs they use to catch wild hogs with had gotten out and were killing our calves. So father come back to the house and told me to get my gun and some extra shells and get in the truck. Well I got my 16 gauge and a pocket full of shells. Pumpkin and I jumped into the truck and down the road we went. There was 7 dogs killing calves father got on one side of the swamp and I on the other and we sent Pumpkin into the swamp. When Pumpkin would run the dogs out we would kill them. Well there was one dog I shot and it run back into the swamp and Pumpkin caught him and had him on a tree that was slanted. I would call Pumpkin to come and the dog would slide down the tree even though he was already dead Pumpkin thought he was still alive because he was moving and would jump on him again. I finally had to go in the swamp and get him or he would have never stopped fighting. Well we killed 6 out of 7 dogs that were killing our calves. Needless to say the neighbors and or family didn't get along anymore. But we didn't have any more dogs killing our cows.

I got to reading where other county's had Jr. Deputy Programs. So, I help put together one in Bonifay. Officer Ard was our Senior Deputy that was over the Jr. Deputies and oversaw what we did. We would ride with the deputies; work at the jail, and work security at the rodeo, all night gospel sing and fairs. We had training meetings once a month. There were eight of us in the group. We wore white uniform shirts, green pants with a gray strip on the leg.

Father got to where he would let me drive the truck to school. We always kept a shotgun and a rifle in the truck gun rack loaded. Mr. Edwards, who was a coach, taught a Hunting safety course. I got to run the clay pigeon throwing trap, because he knows I could shoot. We had some girls that could outshoot the boys in the class.

We had a bully at the school that was on the football team and would always pick on me. I told Ma Segrest and she said something to the principle, but he would not do anything to stop him because he was one of their star football players.

I went to the Sheriff and told him what was happening and the people at the school would not do anything, so this is what happened. The Sheriff gave me a leather slap jack and told me when David the bully came to take my books away from me to give them to him, when he walked up so his hands would be full, then take that slap jack and start whipping him on the head.

Well the next day at school I put my slap jack in the edge of my pants so I could get a hold of it. When I got to school, I went and hunted David before he could catch me off guard. When he came at me, I handed him my books and took out the slap jack and started working on his head. I ran him all the way into the girl's bathroom and embarrassed him. The principal took me into the office and called the sheriff. When he got there the principal said he was going to expel me from school and gave the Sheriff the slap jack and told him he had no right giving me a weapon. The Sheriff told him if he expelled me, he would arrest him for not doing something about David bullying people and him not doing anything to stop it. The principal changed his mind and told us to leave his office. When we walked out the door, the Sheriff gave me back my slap jack, and said I doubt you will need it, but I would have it in case I did. I never had any more problems out of David while in school.

1979

This year was a very busy year, between going to school, helping around the Sheriff's Department as a Jr. Deputy, and working for Ma Segrest. If I remember correctly that year Ma Segrest took me and our Jr. Garden Club members to Mobile, Alabama where we went to the Bellingrath Gardens. The rose garden was in full bloom, the big green house was full of beautiful plants. The whole garden was great to walk through. If you have the chance to go through the home take the tour. The Bellingrath family was part of the Coke Company. There is so much history to learn. Plus, Ma Segrest told us so much about each flower.

Once we were through, we got back on the bus and started back, when we got to a small town called Malbis, Alabama. Ma Segrest had the bus driver to stop at an old Greek Orthodox Church that is there. For a young country boy that was the most beautiful Church I had ever walked into. Because Baptist don't have real nice church's like that. At that point in my life I started exploring other religious groups. I went to Holiness Churches, Methodist, and Catholic Churches. As time went on, I think I have been to every domination of church there is other than devil worshiping. At the age where I am in life, I believe everyone has their own relationship with our creator no matter what your religious belief is. I myself go to a Non-Domination Church, because it's not what's over the door of the church that's going to get you to heaven it's what's in your heart. That's all I'll say about that.

While at the house one day the neighbor that lived in my Uncle Doyle's house he rented (the old Marshall home place) thought the woods from our house called. She was in a panic, she had a small Dotson car and on her way home a big gator was crossing the road, she was afraid to hit it because it might turn her car over. So I got into the truck and went over there. When I got there I found the gator trying to climb the fence into one of our other fields. I took out the 30.6 rifle from the gun rack in the truck. Walked up behind it and shot the gator in the head. When he went down I took a chain from the back of the truck and wrapped it around the gators tail. I turned the truck around and hooked the chain to the truck and drug the gator down the road to her house. When I got there her dog came running out to chase my truck, when it saw the gator it made a flip in the air turning to run the other way.

The lady use to have 5 dogs and she was down to one. I would guess that they had met the gator also. But that dog did not want anything to do with that gator. I pulled up in to her driveway and got out to talk with her. She agreed that it was the gator. And her dog kept peeking out from around the house to see if the gator was still there, it was so funny. I got a measuring tape out of the truck to measure the gator. I looked down and the chain started tightening up, he was still alive. I took the rifle and walked in front of the gator stuck it to his head and turned the gators lights out for the last time. The gator measured out to be 11 foot 8 inches long.

This was a sad year Papa Winter's died from phenomena at a military hospital in Fort Rucker, Alabama. Ma Winter's, Aunt Hank, and I had to plan a funeral. Papa Winter's help build the first Catholic Church in Bonifay. He was the first person to have a funeral at the church and buried on the grounds. I have never helped do a funeral service. A Catholic funeral service will get your legs and knees in shape, from all the standing and kneeling. Their daughter Brenda came down for the funeral. She is big in the Nursing field; she travels a lot. I never saw her again until Ma Winter's funeral.

When I started back to school Ma Segrest ask my mother and father could I move in with her and Doc through the weekdays. The reason for that was Doc had a stroke about 15 years prior to this and his health had started to deteriorate. With her teaching she could not stay up with Doc all through the night to help him use the bathroom and be rested enough to teach during the day. So, they agreed on me moving in through the week and coming home on the weekends to take care of my horse, play with Pumpkin and mow the yard.

1980

W ell 9th grade year came and went; I was busy with the Jr. Deputies and taking care of Doc and Ma Segrest.

I also buried Ma Winter's that year. So, I had to plan a funeral that year for her and I saw Brenda for the last time. Aunt Hank sold the house and moved back to Canada.

This was a rough year. Mother left me with father and moved back to Pensacola, Florida. I tried to kill myself because I did not want to live with him. I took a .22 rifle put it to my head and pulled the trigger. I still have a crease in my forehead where the bullet when because I have a hard head.

Mama Winters, Mother, and Aunt Hank

CHAPTER 2

1981

February that year, I was outside the house feeding and my cousin's wife Jerylan came driving past our house headed to her house after she got off from work. I waved at her and went back to feeding my horse. A few minutes later I heard 3 shots that sounded like from a .22 rifle which is nothing unusual to hear in the country. I went about my normal business and went into the house.

It started raining and storming around 9pm a knock came to the door of the house. It was one of the deputies and they told father to get his gun and come with them. They came back a few minutes later and father said to make coffee. They were using our house as a command post because they had to wait for the FDLE to arrive, someone had shot and killed Jerylan my cousin's wife.

Sometime during the night, it stopped raining and the FDLE when to Jerylan's and did their investigation. They gathered all their evidence, then went to the hospital and did an autopsy on Jerylan.

The next day I went up there and did my own investigation. You could tell that she was first shot at the doorway, because the groceries were still lying in the floor. There is a large puddle of blood next to the coffee table and I looked and saw where the bullet was still in the coffee table. It looked like they had drugged her out of the house and across the yard to her car where they put her into the car.

I went back to my house and called the sheriff's department and told them what I had found in the coffee table to send the FDLE back out to get the evidence.

You could see where the rain had made puddles in the pine straw and blood was gathered. So that showed me that ever who killed her had to struggle to get her into the car waiting so long while she was bleeding out.

Everything quieted down and we when back to normal around the house. But kept my eyes open watching for anyone going by the house or up at Jerylan's house. By the way my cousin's name is Broward we called him Hoodley. He was my father's sister's son from her first marriage.

The FDLE's theory, Jerylan came home from work with her grocery's, got out of the car took her keys and opened the door. Once she opened the door someone shot her with a .22 rifle in the lower part of her back. Jerylan fell to the floor dropping her groceries. The person that shot her come over to her and fought with Jerylan while fighting with her next bullet went into the door. They knocked her to the floor; put their foot on her throat shooting her again in the head with that bullet lodging into the coffee table. Then they took her by the legs and drug her outside face down across the yard to her car, where they put her into her car with her feet over the seat.

Now supposedly her husband (Hoodley) finds her when he comes home from work. Takes her out of her car places her into his truck, drives past our house and goes to our neighbors house the Byres, puts her into one of their cars and drives her to the hospital where she dies.

I have a lot of questions about this. 1) Why would you take her out of her car and put her into your truck? The less movement and faster you get her to the hospital better her chances to live. 2) Why would you drive by our house and know we have medical training plus three vehicles to help get her to the hospital. 3) Why would you stop at the third neighbor's house down the road and move her once again from his truck into one of their vehicles? 4) Why didn't you call the sheriff's department before you left for the hospital?

Three days later I am outside, and I saw a car parked up at Jerylan's house. So, I get my pistol and put it on my hip drive my truck up to the house and ask the two guys there to identify themselves and why were they there? Come to find out they were with the FDLE one guy's name was Jerry, he was the lead investigator. He ask me my theory, and I told him, I showed him everything I had found that they missed. I will tell my theory later and you will understand why.

Four days later after Jerylan's murder a lady that was a nurse in the emergency room with her before she died was found stabbed to death in her house. This is a crazy one. She lived in down town Bonifay. Her house had a 6-foot privacy fence around the whole house with electric fence on the bottom and top of the fence. With three very mean dogs inside of the fence.

My question is, how can someone get into a house that is totally fenced in with three mean dogs and kill her and get out without being bit if they didn't know her? Or she didn't hear the dogs barking to warn her someone was coming in the house if she didn't know them?

Well back to Jerylan, I was at her funeral and it was the first time Hoodley was seen since the murder. I was setting in the car waiting in the funeral procession to start. This was the first time I ever heard the sing with George Jones (He stopped loving her today). Wow, what a day.

Well things started dying down at least we thought it was. The next day another lady that worked at the hospital was found dead. So now we have three people dead that are related to the same thing in my book. What a wild week for the Holmes county sheriff's department.

Now you can hear my theory. Hoodley owed people drug money and the only way they could get their money was to kill Jerylan for the insurance money. The other two ladies were killed because they were in the emergency room when Jerylan was brought in and the killer thought she talked to them, Plus the first lady stabbed her husband was one of the biggest drug runners in Bonifay. Hoodley had someone to set in the field across from their house and wait for Jerylan to come home. When she arrived home with her grocery's they shot her from across the road and the bullet lodged inside her not going through making her fall to the floor. By the time the shooter walked across the road to her, she had gotten up and fought with them making the gun go off, and the bullet going into the edge of the door face. The killer then knocked her to the floor put their foot into her throat holding her to the floor and shot her through the head, where the bullet lodged into the coffee table. Then they flipped her over or she rolled over and they drug her out of the house across the floor over the porch and then through the yard to where her car was parked. They placed her into the car with her head in the seat and feet over the seat. Her husband came home found her, put her into his truck.

Drove her over to his friends that he does drugs with not stopping at our house because we would save her life. And they took their time getting her to the hospital. That's my theory and I'm sticking to it.

Mama & Doc Segrest

Then in March, Ma Segrest told me to go home and spend some time with my Dog and horse. When I got there father yelled from the shop and said Mrs. Segrest called and said to come quick. I had just gotten through playing with Pumpkin and was headed down to the horse pen with some feed, so I just throwed the bucket of feed over the fence to my horse. I jumped into my truck and drove as fast as the truck would run to the Segrest house. When I got there no one was at the house. So, I went back out and got into the truck and headed to the hospital that is at the top of the hill from their house. I run into the hospital asking, "Where was my mama?" Most of the people there knew me from going to the hospital with Doc. They said she had left, and then I started screaming "where is Doc?" They said he was in the emergency room. I walked in the emergency room and he was in the table died.

I ran back out of the hospital and got into the truck and back down the hill to the Segrest house I went. When I got there this time, I found Ma Segrest setting in the kitchen at the table waiting for the water to get hot for her tea. I was crying and she looked at me and said, "Land sakes alive child stop that crying. Go out to the green house and water the flowers and think about everything's Doc has told you through the years." So, I went to the green house crying and watering flowers. And just like Doc was standing there I heard,

"Son never cry for a person when they die because they are in a much better place, cry for them when they are born. I have birthed so many babies that I did not know if they would have food on their table to eat, but when they die, they are so much better off." Well I stopped crying and heard a car drive up, I walked through the garage and it was their son Ralph. He was crying and ask where Mother was? I said Mama is in the kitchen Doc is dead and you need to go to the green house and water the flowers and think of everything Doc has ever told you. So back to planning another funeral.

After everything was over mother saw that I was under a lot of stress and let me come to Pensacola, Florida and live with her. This is my new life. Mother was working at Barn's Supermarket as a cashier, she was living in a one-bedroom small house, and I had to sleep on a small cot. While we were there Terry came to visit. Ramona had divorced Terry because he finally told her he was gay and had a boyfriend. They had already had two kids, Aubri and Jeremy. Terry took them with him, and they traveled the world with his boyfriend Tedo he was the owner of Hanes underwear. Ramona said she could accept loosing Terry to another man, because she could not give him what a man could. Anyway, Terry brought the kids to see their grandmother. The kids sleep with mother, Terry sleep on the couch, and I sleep in the kitchen on my cot. Sometime during the night, I had a bed side visitor; Terry wanted some of what he had gotten years ago. He sucked me dry and wanted more.

I would start the 10th grade at Woodham high School. We moved to live in a trailer in Cloud Nine Trailer Court.

As this year went on at Woodham high I made many new friends and had a great teacher Mrs. Swearington. This teacher helped me so much, she diagnosed me with dyslexia. Now you know why I get side tracked and can't spell worth a shit.

We had a program at the school called the (OJT) On Job Training program. I would go to three classes at school and then to work the remainder of the day. I started at the Escambia County Sheriff's Department as a student investigator. I worked crimes against property. I went to all the pawn shops in Escambia County and picked up all the pawn shop tickets and entered them in the new computer data base. This allowed the other officers to check and see if the property was stolen.

Me when I worked for the Sheriff's Department

The Sheriff's Department had an Explorer law enforcement group Chapter #117. All they did was meet once a week and do military drill marching and setting in a classroom. It was not that fun. I joined the Explorers and was bored to know points end, the other people in the group was bored as well. They would have elections once a year to change out the leaders.

Ramona moved to Pensacola, Florida and started dating a guy in the trailer park Dan. When she dumped him, mother started dating him. Boy we have a screwed-up family. It started getting serious between them and Dan asked mother to marry him.

I was still working in the investigation division of the sheriff's department I was issued my radio call number and my identification card #933. Yes, I had a badge, and was receiving a paycheck working at the Sheriff's Office.

1982

The grandkids want to spend some time with their real grandparents and go on a vacation. So, mother agreed and they when to Disney, when they got back, and mother tried to leave father got drunk and was holding her and the kid's hostage. Mother got word to me, so I went to Bonifay to get her and the kids. I called Ramona and told her to meet me there and what was happening. So, Romana met me down the road from the house and I told her when we drove up to get the kids and put them into the car first. So, when we drove up, we were lucky, father was in the back of the house. So, we grabbed the kids and put them into the car. Father heard what was going on and run into the living room and hit mother knocking her down. Ramona hit father and knocked him over the couch. I told her and mother to get into the car and go. Father looked at the bar where his pistol was laying. I saw his eyes, I told him please put your hand on it and I will have a reason to shoot and kill you. Well I guess that is where I get my crazy from. He put his hand on the gun and I shot him through the side, he fell to the floor and I walked over and put my foot on his hand that the gun was in. I cocked my gun and told him that this was the perfect time to kill him and I would get away with it, but I'm not because we are going to all let him live an ole lonely life and that's how he would die. I took his gun and emptied it; throw the bullets out the door and the gun too. Then I got into the car and drove off. Aubri said, Mama hit grandpa so hard it knocked him over the couch. I said yes, she did. LOL!

While I was driving, I turned my radio on the radio channel the Holmes county sheriff's department was on and call for the sheriff car#1 Drew. I told him I had just shot Shorty (my father) he was holding my mother and grandkids hostage. If he needed me, I would be in Pensacola. Sheriff Drew said, he would go check on him personally. Everyone in Bonifay knew how mean our father was. I never heard anything more about it. Sorry to report he lived through it.

My supervisor over the investigation office was Captain Adrian, he was a great boss. Adrian told me I was an asset for crimes against property division; the computer system was just getting introduced to the sheriff's department. Adrian wanted my idea on how I thought we could catch a lot of people with stolen property. I told him if we were to do a sting operation in pawn shops, like open a fake pawn shop and tell people we will buy any kind of property hot or not. Two months later we had opened a pawn shop.

I was still going to the Explorer meetings and I was voted in as the Captain over the Explorers. The next day I went to the Sheriff Mr. Vince and ask him could I change the Explorer's to the Jr. Deputies so we would not be a part of the Boy Scouts Chapter #117 anymore. I wanted him to allow us to self-train them in every division in the sheriff's office, warrants, dispatch, identification, jail, and ride along with patrolmen. He gave us him blessing and it was on like a chicken bone. Every Jr. Deputy got to work in the area they wanted to specialize in. Now we are getting somewhere and not just setting in a classroom people are really learning something and seeing if they want to really be a deputy as their life job. On some weekends we would go on camping trips, tubing and canoeing. Once the word got out what the Jr. Deputies were doing, we tripled in size.

The pawn shop was going great, we were buying all kinds of stolen property and getting warrants ready to serve on the people selling the hot stuff to us. We were recording them telling us that the property was stolen. Wow, what dummies. The two officers that were working the pawn shop could not believe how well it was working. Wayne and James had been with the sheriff's department for several years and could not believe a new young guy could come up with something that worked so easy. They were kind of jealous.

Mother and Dan got married, my mother was happy once again. I told Dan if he ever put his hands on my mother and hurt her, I would kill him. He promised he would never hit her in anger and try to keep her happy as long as she was alive.

Mother & Dan

I would meet Phillis and Ted their kids were in the Jr. Deputies and they wanted to be Senior Sponsors. They would take us on our field trips and invite everyone over to their house at times. As time went on, they were molesting most all the boys that were in the group.

Ted would ask me to go help him work at their rental houses and while there he would find some young guys to come back where we were working and have sex with them. He took me to the College one time to the bathrooms that was my first experience with a glory hole. (Damn some of those college boys knew how to suck a dick.)

Jim their youngest son and I were friends. We never did anything sexual. But, He did have some friends that come over that his father had already been having sex with. One guy Sonny, Ted told me to go us stairs one day and see what was in Jim's room. So I went up and Sonny was up there in bed, and was laying there with a hard on waiting for me. You can only imagine what took place; he was on the top bunk bed the perfect height to suck a dick.

1983

This is the year that I thought would never arrive. My brother graduated from college cum laude. I'm graduating high school thank the lordly. On our senior trip we went to Tampa Bush Gardens. After we left Bush Gardens we went to Disney for senior night. When we got to our hotel some of the local guys started harassing the girls. Some of the guys come and got me to go help stop them. I had carried my badge and pistol with me, so I told the local guys to please leave the girls alone and I called the local sheriff's department to come deal with them. That night we went to Disney for senior night, we rode the rides and then all gathered in front of the Castle for a concert. The actors from Grease were there to sing and put on a show. We had a great time, when we left Disney me and one of my friends turned out the lights, he got on one side of the bus and I on the other. We both had air pistols and we shot out the streetlights as we went out the gates of Disney. Now Disney has lights with thick glass they can't be shot out. We really turned out the lights that night.

Me and the Girls on Senior Trip

I still had my job at the Sheriff's department. Father bought me a car for my graduation present, well he took it back after he found out mother was remarried, and I didn't want anything to do with him. That's ok I bought my own car and he can't take that away.

I took the J.R. Deputies to Panama City to the Petticoat Junction. It was an Amusement Park with roller coasters, and other rides, plus they had an Old train that took you to a ghost town with gun fights. Lora and the girls all enjoyed the rides plus the ghost town. My father was working at his BBQ stand at the ghost town. We have furnished the horses for the gun fighters for years, so they treated me and the group like VIP guest.

We closed the pawn shop sting operation down. We recovered over three quarters of a million dollars in stolen property and made over 600 arrests. Captain Adrian was a happy man and gave me a raise. I really felt good about myself, I'm 19 just get out of school the Captain over the Jr. Deputy squad and worked investigations. I thought I had life by the tail on a downhill swing.

Well memorial weekend came, and the sheriff's department was short of help. I had the Jr. Deputies to work the beach for gay pride to direct traffic on the beach and crowd control. I stayed at the substation all weekend. I was sleeping in the substation and there were no other deputies on the beach, I was by myself. At around 2:30am dispatch called and said there was a medical emergency at Junk yard hotel. I put my shoes on and got into my patrol car and went to the hotel. A guy came out and told me his girlfriend was in the room. I got out of the car and went into room, the girl was having a seizure and buck naked. I told the guy an ambulance was on the way and I put my ink pin into her mouth. I ask the guy what happened. He said, they were having sex and he thinks her cummer got stuck. I thought I would die laughing, this guy had never saw someone have a seizure; he thought he was really doing her some good.

Then here come trouble, Jerry with the FDLE came to the Sheriff's department and wanted to talk to me. Captain Adrian called me into his office and told me that I didn't have to talk to them if I didn't want to. After talking to Jerry, they wanted me to take a Polygraph test, I agreed to it, and passed it. They named me as a suspect in the murder investigation of Jerylan. Captain Adrian called me back into his office and told me he hated to lay me off but being under investigation I could no longer work at the Sheriff's department. There goes my dream.

I was able to stay as the Captain over the Jr. Deputies because it was not a paid position. Wayne and James the two deputies I had working the pawn shop sting never cared much about me because I came in as a young guy with no experience and pulled off something they didn't come up with and I was successful. They started dogging me, to see if they could make Jerry with the FDLE theory come true. These three people are the type of law enforcement that I didn't want to be. They were trying to hang a murder on me because they were jealous but had no proof.

I contacted my ole school teacher Mrs. Swearington and told her what was going on and she had me to talk to her ex-husband that was one of the best attorney's in Pensacola. He wrote a letter the FDLE and told them to leave me alone or charge me if they had the evidence. Due to them not having any evidence they dropped the harassment. But the Sheriff would not hire me back because of the suspicion. They did not take my badge, or my radio.

1984

Mother and Dan sold the trailer and we moved into my Uncle Woody's house (Laura) he is mother's brother, he got a divorce and wanted mother to take care of his son Chris. While we were staying there Chris was a weightlifter and football kind of guy. Well he pulled a shoulder muscle and mother told him to go take a bath and rub his shoulder with some deep heat. Well I was outside, and mother was in the kitchen cooking. I heard Chris screaming to the top of his lungs. I thought mother was whipping him, I ran into the house to see what was going on. Mother was in the kitchen and said for me to go to the bathroom and see what was wrong with him. When I walked into the bathroom Chris was in the tub splashing water on his privates, screaming hot. Come to find out he had dried off and was rubbing deep heat on his shoulder, when his jock itch kicked in and he scratched with the same hand he just rubbed the deep heat with, and set his balls on fire. I got some lotion and told him to rub the lotion in his balls maybe it would stop burning.

I went to work for Ranger Patrol and Security Agency. I received my Florida Department of Treasury identification. I was assigned to Sandy's bar and Lounge; this place is where all the wild county boys partied. I met Eleanor and she loved to dance; we became very good friends. Boy did we have some humdinger of some fights at the bar. I started off as a sergeant.

I moved out of the house from mother and Dan. I moved in with Eleanor at the 9th Ave. Rain Tree Apartments. She was a very good friend. She worked in a dress shop as a sells person.

Eleanor

I was transferred from Sandy's bar to patrol sergeant where I drove around all night checking on all the businesses throughout Pensacola and other job sites where men were working. One night while on patrol I was at a bar on highway 98, I received a call that there was a fight at the Lady Lillian bar. I jumped into my patrol car and turned in my lights and siren to respond. While driving a car run a stop sign and hit my car. I called and told them to send someone else because I was in a wreck. I got out checking on the person in the other car. He had hit his head on the side of the window, and I was bleeding but not bad. I ask the guy was he ok, he said fuck you. He was so drunk he could not see. I call dispatch and told them to send FHP (Florida Highway Patrol); they ask did I need an ambulance? I told them not at this time. I ask the guy for his I.D. and again he said fuck you. I ask him to step out of his vehicle, when he stepped out, I ask him again, are you OK? Again, he said, fuck you. When he did, I hit him with my flashlight and throwed him on the hood of his vehicle and handcuffed him. When the FHP arrived, it was officer Mat. He said I thought you didn't need an ambulance. I said I didn't, but he tried to leave and resisted arrest. He laughed and said sure I know you, he popped off with you and you whipped his ass. I laughed and said, that's my story and I'm sticking to it.

I was setting in the Brownsville Church parking lot one night and a guy come up and talked to me. After we talked a while, he wanted to suck my dick. So, I took my gun belt off and pulled out my dick. That guy could suck the carom off a trailer hitch. I started stopping at the church parking lot more often.

We also had to watch a few bars downtown Pensacola. Lieutenant Russell worked that beat. He walked the corner of Main and Palafox where he dealt with Trader John's Bar, Quaside Inn strip club, Pelicans Nest Bar, and the Red Garder. He wanted to trade jobs with me and take over patrol and I walk the bars downtown. So I had to learn the area and people. The first night I went down for training Lt. Russell told me to wear my riot helmet, and I wanted to know why. He said that the people down here would sneak up behind you and hit you in the head with bottles. Understand, Russell is almost 300lbs and 6-foot-tall, I am 145lbs and 5'8" tall, a small difference. Well I choose not to wear a helmet because it restricts my vision and head movement.

Okay, let me tell you a little bit about the bars, Trader John's is a Military bar, Quaside Inn is a strip bar with Vietnamese girls, Pelicans Nest is a black dancing bar, and the Red Garder is a gay show bar.

Well after I was trained, I took over and worked the area 3 nights a week, plus all big holidays. The owner of the Pelicans Nest ask us to stop people from standing in the entrance doorway. So, every so often I would have to tell some of the people to either go inside, or go down the street or go to jail. Most people would do as I ask be then you would have the drunken asshole that would want to try you. I would give them a choice, they could go down the street, go to the hospital or the hospital and jail. Most of them would go down the street. After working down there for about a month I was checking one of the parking lots that have buildings on three sides, so there's only one way in and one way out. While checking this parking lot I looked up and saw about 15 people with sticks, chains, and pipes across the entrance of the parking lot. It was some of the people that I had dealt with in front of the Pelicans Nest that didn't like me telling them to move. Well I drew my pistol and dropped it to my side and shinned my flashlight toward them. I ask them what they were doing. They said they were taking back over downtown and was going to run me off. I raised my pistol and told them to disperse or they could get shot. They said I only had 6 bullets and there were lots more of them. I said, but which 6 wants the first 6 bullets. I called over my radio 933 (I still had me Sheriff's Dept. radio) to control officer needs assistance shots fired at Palafox and Main. Then I started shooting, people were running everywhere. I shot three and other officers rounded up about 10 more that we arrested.

After that night I had very little trouble out of the people at the Pelicans Nest bar. About 4 weeks later I had a few guys that didn't know me to stand on the door and I walked up and said gentlemen we need to find some other place to stand, either go inside or down the road. One guy said I'm from Mobile and crackers don't tell me what to do, I stopped and stared at him. One of the guys that knew me told him, you better leave that crazy son-of-a-bitch alone he will shoot you and not think twice. The guy apologized and walked off.

In the 80's we were still having problems with gay bashing. Every so often we would have a problem with someone jumping on people in the parking lots. The Red Garder was where I met one of my first boyfriends. He looked just like George Michael; his name was Doug. Doug worked as a bar back and sometimes bartender. He had a bad drug habit this was when people were learning how to make meth. Colan was a roommate of Doug's and they would make meth and use it.

One night while working down town Sonny came down town and was in the club. When I started home after 2am Sonny was drunk and wanted me to take him home. He got into the car and we started home when I turned onto his street he ask where was I going? I said you wanted me to take you home. He said No, your house. So I took him home with me and he sure turns into a wild bottom boy when he is drunk.

Doug and I stayed friends but he was a drug addict and I could not deal with him. So, I met Mickey, I thought this would be my soul mate for life. He was related to President Carter; he was the manager of the Family Dollar store there in town. I use to take him lunch a lot of days. One day while we were eating upstairs looking for shop lifters, I had thrown what we didn't eat into the dumpster. I looked out the back window and saw a lady with two small kids eating out of the dumpster what we had thrown away. I told Mickey I would see him later and went down to talk to the lady. I had my uniform on and she thought I was going to take her to jail. I started talking to her and told her she was not going to jail. So, I had her to get into my car, she sure didn't want to do it because she still thought she was going to jail but I talked her into going with me. I drive to Quincy's Steak house where my sister Pat worked. I told her to get out and let's eat, she said she had no money and I told her I didn't ask if she did have money. So, we went in and Pat comes over, I told her what was going on. So, she and Peggy one of the other waiters took the little baby. I took the little boy who was about 4 years old and the lady to get something to eat. After we set down Pat brought the baby over, they were feeding it some soup. She wanted me to look at some sores on the baby's body. They were round sore's that had a look burns. I ask the mother what was wrong with the baby, she started crying. I told her that if she didn't tell me she would be going to jail for child abuse. Well she cracked and said her husband worked out of town and when he came home, he would get drunk and if the baby started crying, he would put his cigarettes out on her. I came close to blowing my cool.

I told her I would make her a deal. If she would call me when her husband came home, I would get her some food for the house and not have her arrested for child abuse for not reporting what happened. She agreed, so I took her to Sack and Save and got some milk, cereal, bread and sandwich meat. Then I took her home so I would know where she lived. I gave her my phone number and told her to call as soon as her husband comes to town.

A few weeks went by and I was in bed when my phone rang, it was her. I told her to hang up and don't say anything. I got dressed into my dark close with a dark face mask. I put my gun belt on and got my small rifle and went and sat on their front porch. A few hours later her husband came outside and when he did, I put my rifle under his neck and told him to get on his knees. I put handcuffs on him and a hood on his head. I made him get into my car and I took him out into the woods where an old barn was. I tied him up inside the barn and left to get a cigar and a lighter. When I came back, I burned him all over his body just like he did the baby even on his dick so he would remember not to have any more kids. He was screaming wanting to know why I was torturing him, I only said remember your baby. When I got through, I took the handcuffs off and untied him, but left the hood on. I told him if he took the hood off or stuck his head out of that building before an hour was up, I would kill him. When I left, I called Captain Adrian and told him what the deal was; he arrested the guy for child abuse and the guy plead guilty to 3 years in prison.

October was here and it was time for the Bonifay Rodeo. Sonny said he wanted to go with me. So we took a tent and camped out. On Saturday night after the rodeo was over I went to the tent and Sonny had been out drinking. When he came into the tent and lay down he stripped down naked and got into the bed with me. He backed his ass up and told me to stick my dick in and let it get warm. So I did, I rolled him over and gave him all 10 1/2 inches as deep as I could give him. Some people came walking by the tent and looked into the window of the tent and saw us and started laughing. I didn't slow up, fact was it made me nut fast. He makes a good person to go camping with.

I was out on patrol and Dan was working as a guard at Dr. Pimiento who was an abortion doctor. It was Christmas week and they had received boom threats so we had to keep his office guarded around the clock. On Christmas night someone got by Dan and set a boom in the Office and blew the doctor's office up.

1985

The second week in January Dr. Pimiento opened up a temporary office next to Sacred Heart Hospital. John a abortion protestor, was dumb enough to put a add in the paper saying that he was going to going to come into the office and take all the woman out. Well did I have a surprise for him? I had four undercover officers in the office waiting on him.

I was in uniform standing out in from of the office; I told the secretary that I would let John into the office. Once he comes into the office she needed to ask them to leave, after she ask him to leave the third time we would arrest him. Well John came walking up and I stepped out of the way so he could come in the door. John had three other people with him, his daughter, Son, and some little old lady. After the Secretary ask them to leave the third time the undercover grabbed the son and the daughter and I grabbed John. When we stayed out the door with them the news cameras where in front of the door. I head butted the camera with Johns head and told them to get out of the way; they were interfering with a Law Enforcement investigation. Then I handcuffed him on the wall outside the office. A patrol car was pulling up just in time, where we place him and his two kids. Somehow the little old lady snuck out and got away.

That night I was on national news arresting John and his kids. My Aunt called and was mad that I had arrested them. I told her that I didn't care for people getting abortions but what John did was against the law and I had to do my job. She could like it or not, she did have to talk to me anymore.

On Valentines weekend I would go help Bud at the Flower Shop we had over off Fairfield Dr. in the New Warrington area. Now you want to see a sight, I had on a pair of hot pink shorts. We set a table up by the road and I would run out into traffic and sell flower arrangements to people at the Stop sign. I sold so many flowers we ran out of flowers and we had to go into the trash and get broken flowers and stick floral wire in the flower to make them stand up and put in the arrangements. That was some funny crap.

Mickey and I had our ups and downs. We got a house on Scenic Highway and I had to go out of town to pick up a person. I got back home early and was going to surprise him. I was going to sneak into the house, but he had the door dead bolted so I couldn't get in. So, I called the house and when he answers, I told him to open the door I got back home early, he said he couldn't. So, I climbed up to the balcony and busted in the glass door. There was a guy come out of our bedroom naked, I pulled my gun and told him to stop. Mickey was on the phone calling the sheriff's office, and he screamed don't shoot him. I said your right he doesn't have a key to our house to get in without you letting him in. In a few minutes a K-9 officer pulled up and turned his dog out. I yelled to the officer, is that you Garry? He said yes, I said put your dog back into the car because if he bits me I'm going to shot him. I walked over and told him I had everything under control, and he could leave. After he left, I had a talk with Mickey and he decided to move back to Rome, Georgia with his family.

Mickey

I stayed in Pensacola and dealt with the bars. I was walking around one night and there was a noise in the parking lot behind the Red Garden, when I got there three guys were trying to beat up a drag queen name Tony. He was knocking those boys out every time one would come at him with his purse. Matt a guy who was Highway patrol officer was walking with me and we went to help Tony. I took my night stick and Matt had an aluminum baseball bat. When we got through with the guys I told them I was not going to take them to jail, I was going to send them back home and let them explain how they got their asses beat to everyone by a bunch if gay men. That little talk with them basically put a stop to the gay bashing downtown Pensacola.

A few months later they ask me to help train a new young guy downtown. So, I had him downtown showing him where everything was and introducing him to all the people downtown. We were in the Red Garder standing in the back bar when I saw out the corner of my eye a person hitting someone with a pool stick at the pool table area. I and Kennedy ran back to the pool table area. I picked up the girl and ask her was she Okay? I told Kennedy to take her out the back door and meet me at the front door I was going after the other person. I walked off into the dance area where it was shoulder to shoulder. I pushed my way through until I got to the person who had assaulted the girl and I grabbed her by the hair and she pushed me, when she did I grabbed her into a head lock using her as a body blocker to get to the front door. Once I got her outside the door, I bent her over into the brick flower planter that was about waist high. While I was handcuffing her, Kennedy got her other hand and was handcuffing it; I only heard two clicks in the handcuff. I told him he needed to tighten her handcuff. He said but she's a lady. I told him to go get the car because she was going to jail. When he drove up there were cars parked on the side of the street, so he had to park in the street, and we had to load her in the back of the car on the driver's side. Once we passed the parked car and was in front of our patrol car in the street. Kennedy had her by her left arm and I had her right arm. She slipped her hand out of the handcuff and came around and hit Kennedy in the face causing him to lose two teeth and falling to the pavement. I grabbed her by the shoulder and tripped her onto the pavement and sat on her back hitting her head into the pavement. I told her to put her hands behind her back and I would stop. I rehandcuffed her and stood her up. By then Kennedy had gotten up spitting blood out wanting to whip her ass. I stopped him and told him, you forgot she's a lady. Well we got her into the back of the car, and she started kicking the door. I opened the door and told her if she didn't behave herself I was about to make her be a good girl. I tied her feet together and put her seatbelt on; she rode to the jail like a nice girl. I told Kennedy to treat everyone the same, when you handcuff someone you go to the fat meat so they can't get loose and hurt you.

A few weeks later I was told to train Kennedy to take my place working downtown, I would be going to a different bar to work on weekends and patrol daring the week. The new bar is called Faces. One of my best friends worked there, He and I were partners in a flower shop, and His name is Bud. He was the front door person who took money and checked I.D.'s.

While working at Faces they had a show bar, Cruse bar and a restaurant. One-night Bud told me to meet him in the restaurant they had hired a new cook her name was Debbie. Bud and I were in the restaurant and we were talking to Debbie, Bud ask her what her whole name was, and she replied, Pussy. I thought he and I would roll out of our seats.

One night while on patrol I was downtown talking with Kennedy and I received a call from one of the construction sites. They said they could hear a lady screaming for help. So, I headed that way with lights and siren so I could get there fast. On my arrival the person at the job site was not licensed to carry a weapon and he had a shotgun walking around. I told him to put up the gun he would wind up killing someone. He said there's a lady in the drain system screaming for help, I told him I would deal with it. So, I went down into the drainpipes to try and find the lady that was screaming, sure enough I found her. It was a mama cat meowing and it sounded like a woman screaming. This guy was about to blow up the world over a cat.

A few weeks later while out on patrol I and my patrol partner John a great big black guy stopped at the Nite owl after hours bar. Ms.Gaynail told me there was a guy upstairs asleep and she wanted him out. So, I left John talking to her and I went to deal with the problem. When I got upstairs the guy was asleep with his head on the table. By law you cannot sleep in a bar with your head on a bar or table. So, I bumped the guy on the shoulder with my flashlight waking him up and I ask him to stay awake or get up and leave. Well he was not happy that I had waked him up, and he told me to fuck you. So, I told him to just get up and leave. I went to give him by the hand to get up and he grabbed me by my watch band, and I could not get him off. So, I reached and got my hay hook out of my pocket and hooked him into the top of his hand and pulled him to me so I could lean him against the rail and handcuff him. Well that was a bad idea, because he fell over the rail and I could not get my hay hook out of his hand or turn loose. He dragged me over the rail We hit the dance floor and I landed on top of him and it knocked him out, so it gave me enough time to put handcuffs on him. When he came to, I told him to get up and walk out to the car. He was hardheaded and told me to carry him to the car, now this guy is about 240lbs. and I was only 145lbs. so I'm not carrying him anywhere, so I told him to stand up I would get him there. So, I grabbed him by his handcuffs and took the hay hook and popped it into him ass and he was hitting the ground about every other step. When I got him to the car, I leaned him over the trunk of the car and ask John to shake him down.

This guy started telling John that I was harassing him, and I was a racist. John threw him over the trunk of the car into oncoming traffic. I jumped out into traffic stopping cars so they would not run over him, I grabbed the guy up and told him if he did shout his mouth that black man was going to kill him. John my partner did not like to hear anyone talking racist crap. While this was going on a big crowd of people had started together. I ask them to disperse and we had a loud mouth that wanted to have people to try and take us. I walked over and grabbed the loudmouth leader and handcuffed him. I walked over to the car and told the other guy that if he would get a cab and go him, I would let him go because his loudmouth friend was going to jail.

Well it's Christmas time at the flower shop. I was back out by the road selling flowers by the road. One day Bud and I were in the shop making some arrangements and we saw a car drive up so Bud said let's sing some crazy Christmas carols. So Bud started singing, Hark the hair lip angels sing, Glory to the new born king. Then said LEON, LEON, LEON. Oh hell the music is upside down. NOEL, NOEL, NOEL. They person thought we had slipped off out rockers and started laughing.

CHAPTER 3

1986

This is changing my life forever. I was hanging out with some of the guys that I met that went to the bar. A guy named Steve who owned the Stop and Go shop in Pensacola, wanted me to loan him some money and help him with a few deals.

I was on patrol and doing security at a Hotel on Hwy. 29 that a lot of truckers stayed at. Steve wanted me to help him steal some cars and take to Texas and sale. Well, they would leave the keys in these new cars that they were delivering to the dealership. I would take one of the two sets of keys; I would write down the deal ship off the sticker where the car would be delivered and give Steve the keys. Before they could inventory the cars, he and someone else would take the cars so they wouldn't know that the car was missing and take them to Texas or some place and sell them. Fast good money.

Doug and Colan were friends with Steve. They caused me to stop working with Ranger Patrol because they wanted me to help Steve move the cars and other things. Yes, with Mickey out of my life I went crazy for anyone I could stick a dick into.

I started working for a gas station and was doing the bank deposits. So Colan came up with the idea I should act like I got robbed and hand off the money to him and Doug. So, I did! Doug and Colan went to New Orleans and wanted me to meet up with them there. We met up and partied with the money that I had given them.

When I returned to Pensacola I was questioned more by the Sheriff's Department. Funny thing it was the two officers that I had running the pawn shop sting operation, James and Wayne. They had me to come to the Sheriff's Department and talk with them. James illegally searched me and took my Sheriff's Department Identification and Badge and never gave me a receipt for them. They tried to act like I was impersonating an officer and threatened me with arrest. Well, working with the sheriff's department I knew their tricks. They released me and I went home.

Well Bud turned the Flower shop into a video store. I would go set and rent videos. A black family that lived down the road would come in all the time to rent videos. One day we got a phone and it was the black lady, she asked Bud do you have any of these videos? Her son was taking black history at school and they wanted him to watch the videos for his home work. Well Bud said yes I have some of them send him on down and I will get them ready for him. Well when the kid got there he said, Hello Mr. Bud and Lonnie how are you'll today. We said we are doing well, here are your video's you mother wanted you to have. He said, yes I have to watch them for my black history class, I don't know why I have to watch them, I've been a Nigga all my life. I thought Bud and I would roll out the door laughing. That was some funny shit.

A few weeks later another shipment of cars comes through and I get 3 sets of keys. Steve, Colan and I took the cars to San Antonio Texas and sold two of them Colan didn't want to sell the sports car he had he wanted to drive it around like a dumbass. Steve had a guy who was our contact there and he wanted us to burn his house down so he could collect the insurance money. Steve and I went that night and burned the place to the ground. The fire department said that was the hottest fire they had ever seen. It burned everything in that house but the air ducts for the air conditioning.

We stayed with a friend of Colan's (Brian) that he met at the Paper Moon bar. I met several guys while I was there in San Antonio. One guy who was Latino, another guy who was very sweat, but I didn't want to be with someone because I was still hooked on Mickey. The other guy I met was a guy Colan had brought back to the apartment with 6 other guys they were running a train on each other that night. He came into the living room and set with me. We had sex with each other, and he never left. Come to find out he was married and had two kids; he and his wife were school teachers. He ask me to go with him and get him more clothing. When we got there, we had sex in every part of their house, Shower, Kitchen, both bedrooms, and shower again. I guess he wanted to get caught by his wife. We started out of the house and a lady came over to the car yelling and telling him not to leave and started beating on my car. I told her if she hit my car one more time, I would deal with her in a different way, if he wanted to stay, he could, but don't hit my car anymore. Well, he came with me and didn't leave until I left Texas. I must admit he was good in bed, he said he could not sleep without my dick deep inside of him. I guess he was going to have to learn how to sleep without me.

Terry & Tedo

42

Steve and I left Colin in Texas and went back to Pensacola, 777 miles. When I got back to Pensacola my sister Ramona wanted me to take her to North Carolina where Terry and Tedo were living so she could see the kids. So, on the road once again. We drove to where Terry was living, and I stayed the night with them. I slept in the living room on the flood, Ramona slept with the kids, and Terry with Tedo. I woke up to my old childhood feeling with Terry sucking my dick.

Ramona stayed there with Terry and the kids and I left. I stopped in Rome Georgia to see Mickey. When I got there, he was nowhere to be found. I spoke to his mother and told her what hotel I was staying at. Around 9pm a knock came to my door and it was Mickey. While we were having sex, someone knocked on the door and acted really sketchy. When we got through what we were doing Mickey left. I took an hour nap and left myself heading back to Pensacola.

When I got to Pensacola Steve told me we had to leave the sheriff's department was looking for us. It was the first week in October, so we met Eleanor and Joey at the Bonifay Rodeo. We did the rodeo for three days and Joey said his old boss was being a dick to him and made a bank deposit at the bank around 2pm on Sunday. Steve and I went to Dothan the next day to see if we could get that money and give him some respect to his employees. Well we didn't get the money, but he learned some respect.

We went to the Pizza Hut on the circle and got something to eat. While we were setting there eating Steve ask me if I had my gun on me? I said if I have my pants on, I have a gun. So, when we went to the counter to pay, Steve told me to show my gun and he told the lady to give us the money. Well we walked out and got into the car, I drove, and we made it over 10 miles before we had a patrol car behind us. The officer turned his lights on, and I pulled over in front of a church. The people were just getting out of church. The officer came up to the car with his gun out of his holster. He ask me to step out of the car and I did. Steve stayed in the car and tried to hide his gun, when another patrol car pulled up and pulled him out of the car. He told them it was all my idea. When they found my gun and badge, they broke my shoulder and busted my head. They handcuffed me and took me to the car and throwed me into the back of a patrol car. One officer said that they should have killed me. Well they took me to the hospital where the nurse seemed to have felt sorry for me. She bandaged my head and put my arm on a sling.

They took me to the city jail where there was a set of bunk beds enough room to stand by the bed and there was a toilet that looked like it had never been cleaned and it stunk. I had my arm in a sling and I had to get on the top bunk. While that was taking place with me, Steve was in the office singing to them like a bird. I stayed in the city jail for three days where they beat me, and then they moved me to the county jail. That's where I met officer Woodham; he thought we might have been kin. The cell I was in had two bunk beds. There were two black guys that took the bottom beds and a young guy on the other top bed. We would talk off and on, one night the young white guy came over to my bed and set, we got to talking and the next thing I knew he was sucking my dick and then wanted me to fuck him. Well the light was out so it didn't take me long to nut in him.

I went to court in the next few weeks and they told me if I didn't take a plea deal, they had Steve to testify against me and if they found me guilty, they would give me the death penalty. Well I thought about what they said, and I told the attorney I would take the deal. I went before judging White and he said I should have known better to be involved in something like that being a Law Enforcement officer, and he was going to make an example out of me. He sentenced me to life in the Alabama state prison.

While I was there Jerry FDLE came up to talk to me once again. He would not give up trying to get me to say I killed Jerylan. (People this is how they clear cases by getting people that did not commit the crime to say that they did it, they hounded me for 6 years and ruin my life.) Even though I passed their Polygraph test, it was in his head that I killed her even though I told him her husband had done it.

In December they took me to Kilby, which is the Alabama processing center for all men inmates. You are treated like cattle; you come into the receiving area, all your clothing is taken from you. They make you shave, take a shower, and then they spray you for crabs and lice. You receive a set of clothing, shirt, pants, socks, underwear, and shoes. They try to degrade you so you will humble yourself. Then they issue you two sheets, a blanket, a wash cloth, a towel, laundry bag, and lock. I was placed in a very small two man cell. The guards walked around with sticks that drug the floor, Riot sticks to intimidate you more. Until I was processed, then they put me into a cell block with about 120 other inmates. We had only 45 minutes to shower and only had 4 shower heads to bath under, so we had to share a shower if we were going to stay clean. Some people would only bath once a week so you could guess what they smelt like. I could remember going through the classification process. They test you for all types of disease, check your teeth, give you mental health test, and tested you on how much education you had. It's almost like going to a blue collar job interview. Once that is all done then you wait, they class you to which prison you can go to. And you wait for your transfer to that prison.

1987

In January I was woken up around 2am and told to pack my clothing I was on the next chain going out that morning. Even though you are searched when you come into the prison, you're searched again when you leave. They handcuff you and leg chain you before they put you on a bus. You have no clue of where you are going until you get there. Well 4 hours later I arrived at Limestone Correctional Facility in the north corner of Alabama. Now I am 345 miles away from my mother and family. Again, you are stripped of your clothing, and searched, you receive 3 sets of shirts, pants, underwear, socks, pair of Brogans, a pillow case, 2 sheets, a blanket, a towel, a wash cloth, a laundry bag, and a lock. Then you are assigned to a dorm and bed where you will sleep. They tried to place me into the law enforcement dorm where all the Alabama officers and correction officers are housed. I told them that no one knew me in Alabama as a law enforcement officer, so I wanted to be in population.

If you can picture this place, the main office is half mile from the dorms; the chow hall is a half mile from the dorms. There is NO shelter over the sidewalks, so you're in all the elements if you go outside for anything. Limestone houses all the law enforcement officers and all the inmates that have HIV. Yes, they are all housed separate from everyone else. The dorms were setup with A and B sides, each side had two-man cells and beds in the day room. The prison is very overcrowded.

I was assigned to a bed out in the day room in the dorm. I was assigned to the farm. Understand I still had my arm in a sling. We were waking up at 4am every morning to eat breakfast, at 6am we were run out of the dorms to the check out area for the farm squads. The guards were on horseback with shotguns and you had to walk in two's side by side in a line, there were normally 30 inmates to a squad. We would walk to the fields and take buckets and pickup rocks out of the fields. At 10:30am we would come back into the camp where we had to be stripped searched so we could eat. At 1pm we had to be back at the check out for the farm once again, we would stay out and work picking up rocks until 4pm. Officer Bell was my shotgun boss, they say that she could out shoot every man at Limestone. We would return to the camp to be stripped searched and go eat our supper. Then we would go to our dorms to shower and sleep. This would take place everyday but weekends and holidays. Now on Sundays and Holidays we only received two meals, breakfast and supper. If you missed them, you went hungry if you didn't have someone to send you money for your PMOD account.

I met a young guy I thought was very good-looking name Zack. I would share some of my food I would get from the store. Several months passed and the doctor took my sling off my arm. Well one day he invited me to his cell to eat, he didn't stay in the day room like I did. While I was in there a black guy came into the room and Zack stepped out and closed the door. This black guy thought he was going to have sex with me without my approval (rape). Well, no one knew I was law enforcement so I could fight, but that guy learned that night I beat him so bad he was knocking on the door trying to get Zack to open the door so he could get out. I never spoke to Zack again after that day.

I would not get a lot of visits, but Eleanor would come up sometimes and Mother came to see me I think three times the whole time I was there. But Eleanor surprised me one weekend; she brought Mickey to see me. I was very happy, but very embarrassed. It was so good to see him.

Mickey

I was woken up after being there for about three months and told to pack my things. When I got to the back gate there was an out of state transfer van to take me to Pensacola. They took me to Texas and picked up and dropped off people, Mississippi, and Georgia. I traveled for two days none stop on that van. Finally, I told the drivers how to get to Pensacola through the back roads so I could get off that damn van. When I got to Pensacola, they took me to the Escambia Jail where I was a law enforcement officer. This was crazy; I was treated badly until I called them out and called the sheriff and told him how I was being treated. The cell they put me in was with a black guy that thought he could bully me and make let him use my phone time I had. He told me if I didn't let him use the phone he would beat me up. Well I thanked him for the warning. I went back to my cell and full some milk carton full of pee and shit. Jerry FDLE wanted to question me more, he would not give up. I told him I would not talk to him anymore to call the transfer back and send me back to prison. That would be the last time I see Jerry. Sure enough when I got back from seeing Jerry the black guy carried out his threat. When he come into my cell to fight I dodged the punch and hit him, I grabbed the milk carton with pee and hit him in the face. The pee went into his eye and he was blind, he was swinging but not hitting anything. I took the milk carton with shit in them and hit him on both sides of his head. By then the officer in the cubical come to the door and I walked down. He opened the door and I walked out, the officer took me to the infirmary to have me checked for injury. They went back to get the black guy. I told the nurse what happened and she said she would keep me with her so she would not have to go deal with the guy that had shit all over him. When I had gotten back to the cell other inmates had cleaned my cell, because the black guy had been threaten them too, so they were glad for what I did. A few days later the out of state transfer van came and got me. It was my two friends. They didn't even handcuff me. I was taken straight to Limestone, when we got to the back gate of the prison, they handed me a pair of cuffs and told me to put them on so they would not get into trouble.

Well, as time went on, I put in a request to get a two-man cell so I would have a room to sleep in and a little privacy. Now understand our beds only have a box to store our belongings that is 8 inches deep, 3-foot-wide, and 2-foot width. I got a room and my roommate was David. He was an ok guy; He work in the ACI industry, but he had a drug problem. After about three weeks one night I woke up with him sucking my dick and I acted like I was still asleep. He pulled the blanket off me and started riding my dick I never acted like I woke up. I just laid there and enjoyed the ride. I guess after a few months he found someone he liked and was moved to another dorm. I got another roommate. I put in for a transfer to the south end of the state so I could see my mother because she was having health problems.

1988

n February I was transferred to Kilby for a layover, and the next morning I was transferred to Fountain Correctional Facility (The Bottom). This would be my home for the next 5 years. Back to the same ole process, off with the clothing and receive new. Officer Johnson was over the laundry, He gave us our 3 sets of clothing, socks, underwear, bed sheets, face cloth, and Towel. Then we received our bed assignment and Job assignment. This is where I met Capt. Angeles and Assistant Warden Ross, where they did the orientation. This is where they tell you what they expect of you and what they can do for you. Mr. Ross's speech was, "Gentlemen welcome to the bottom, and I know that you might have been a gator on the street, but I'm the only gator around here. The courts sentenced you to do time and I don't care what your here for, our job is to provide security on these fences and peace down this hall. You can go down that hall and do all the drug, drank, screw all the boys and act like a fool if you want to, but we have a place that we can put you and control you. Now, if you want to help yourself, we have schools that can get you an education, and we will help you anyway we can. But you have a choice to go down that hall and do as you wish."

Captain Angeles would give his speech. He was from the Philippines, very good guy and (you will hear a lot from him as time goes on.) Then they would have one of the classification officers to speak and tell you that every 6 months you would have an annual and semiannual review to see if you are eligible for any changes in your status, like custody or transfers.

Well they would wake you up every morning for breakfast around 4am. We would walk into the chow hall and get into a line, pick-up our tray and walk down the food line to receive what food they had to offer, get a spoon or drink and go set down. Once you finish eating you take your tray and dump the tray into the slop barrel, then put your tray into the wash room so it could be cleaned. When you start out the chow hall you would get searched to make sure you have no food going out of the chow hall and no metal spoons to make a knife.

If you needed to take medication you could go to the infirmary to get your pills or go back to your dorm. Once you get back to you dorm, make your bed so you will be ready to go to the checkout areas at 6am. When the shift changed at 6am they would count, and once the count was clear, everyone other than the dorm cleaners had to go out of the dorm for checkout. Some people went to the farm gate for checkout and others would go to the Trade School gate.

The sergeant over the farm was Sgt. W. Hall. He was the most dangerous office at the prison. He had a history of inmates escaping and never being seen again. He was also known as a sharp shooter. He was known to deal with problem inmates. If someone missed the back gate Sgt. W. Hall would put them in the back of his truck and tell them if they tried to jump out he would consider it as an escape and kill them on the spot. The Dog Wardens where somewhat as bad as Sgt. W. Hall, but they would bring you back alive if you didn't resist to bad. Not saying you wouldn't get the hell beat out of you.

I worked on the farm for 2 weeks until lieutenant Williams found out I could type a little and read my background. Then I was moved to the job as the inmate clerk. My duties were finding inmates when they were needed, type the bed assignment rooster, typing the daily logs, typing transfer orders, and keeping up with the inmate count.

During this time I met Robin who was an inmate that repaired radios, and was in welding school, and loved to suck dick and get fucked. He and I would have sex anywhere and everywhere, Library, Law Library, shower, under our beds, out at the school in the attic of the buildings. He was a nice and fun guy, but we were young so sometimes you had to have more than one person to keep up with your sex needs. I met Radar and his boyfriend Brian. Brian was some kind of fine. He worked out a lot and read books. Brian and I would hook-up every so often. Then you had William, he was a nice guy no extra qualities just good to have sex with.

Well, the days went by and things as always happen in prison. We had people try to escape, stabbings, Drugs, and Alcohol everywhere. I will teach you some prison language.

Home Boy - Someone who is from the town you lived in out of prison.

Julep - Alcohol that is made in prison with anything that will ferment.

Mule - a person that puts drug up their butt and brings it into the prison.

Punk - a person that lets someone fuck them.

Gunsell - is a punks, punk.

Chain - is inmates that are being transferred.

Zoom Zoom & Wham Wham - is food from the store.

Ole G - An old man in prison.

Chow call - Go eat.

Pill Call - Go get your medication at the infirmary.

Oh, now - To get someone's attention.

Sissy boy - Female acting homosexual male, Bottom.

Boy - See sissy.

Fuck Sissy - See sissy.

Man - Butch acting homosexual male, Top.

Real talk - No lie.

Keep in it 100 - To tell only the truth.

180 - To do an about face, to turn one's life around.

Be 21 - To take responsibility for their actions.

Snitch - A rat, or to tell on someone.

DooWop - A desert made with made with snack food from the prison store.

Sham - A drink made from instant coffee, some other drink like, cool aid or soda.

No show - synthetic marijuana.

Flocka - A drug that is basically made from drains cleaner and can cause short term paralysis, brain damage or even death. It's widely available in prison do to its potency and low cost.

Skit runner - A person who calls people on the outside from a contraband cell phone to run scams on them for money, sometimes to extort another inmate's family in exchange for not harming them.

Mental Health - A crazy person.

Slides - Plastic or foam rubber sandals intended to be worn in the shower.

Shit Jacket - Stainless steel toilet.

Shank - A DIY knife or stabbing weapon.

Iron - See shank.

Fire - Another word for shank.

Is fire - Something really good?

Shoot - To stab someone.

Car - An am/fm radio.

Cadillac - An amped up modified am/fm radio.

Bald head - Someone with no hair.

Oh now Bald head - To get a person with no hairs attention.

Turn - a fight.

Bumpin - See to turn.

Bumpin fucked up - To fight vigorously and with great skill.

Bomb - A package of contraband usually launched over the fence.

Shot out - To have brain damage or someone not real bright.

Crash out - To do something incredibly stupid that results in major consequences.

Crash dummy - Someone who repeatedly crashes out.

Jumpin - Something good or (see fire).

Fire your ass up - To slap the shit out of someone.

Cappin - Shouting at someone in perceived anger.

Item - Unit of barter and trade cost .65 to $1.00.

Top - Unit of barter and trade which is valued between 4-5 items.

Bag - Unit of barter and trade which is valued between 5-6 items.

Run a store - Someone rune a store when they buy a bunch of items for the intention of reselling at interest or for credit.

Coffee Ball - An items worth of instant coffee, about 2-3 table spoons.

Top Ball - An items worth of prerolled top tobacco, between 4-5 cigarettes.

Paper Ball - An items worth of cigarette papers, about 5 papers.

Match Ball - An items worth of matches, about 4 books.

Freeworld - The world outside of prison.

Free world food - Food not sold in the prison store, brought in either by a church ministry or as contraband through ADOC staff.

Well as the year went by I learned more and more of how things worked on the other side of the badge. If a inmate was a problem inmate they would put them in lock-up, if they steal acted crazy they would take them to the basement of the prison an strap them to the barrel. This was a 55 gallon barrel full of water that was on saw horses with straps built into the sides. They would bend them over the barrel straps their hands to the saw horses, pull his shirt off and beat them with a strap that was leather 4 inches wide and 2 foot long attached to a base ball bat handle. After about three or four hits from that they would humble themselves.

Understand the Bottom was what they call a working farm. They raised Horses, Pigs, Cows, and had gardens with all the vegetables from peppers, cucumbers, squash, potatoes, peas, beans, corn, and other vegetables. Some of them were what they called money crops, where they would sell the crops to the markets of canning companies. They sold the calves to beef processing companies. I also saw some cows get loaded on trailers that belonged to officers.

Well it is Christmas time and I'm in the Shift commander's office typing the shift logs and Captain Hatfield walks into the office. Now this Captain had been with the department of corrections for over 40 years. If he said it you better do it Officer or inmate. He had NO problem kicking an inmate in the ass or officer. He looked at me and told me to come with him. I looked over at the Lieutenant and he said go and don't ask questions. We walked up front to the cubicle where all the keys to the prison were kept. Officer Chancy was in the cub and he told her to give him the 203 key. He walked over to a door and unlocked it;

the room was packed with Christmas packages. He handed me the key and told me to write all the names down that were on the boxes. When I was finished to lock the door back and turn the key back into the officer in the cub. About that time an inmate walked up and Captain Hatfield kicked him in his ass. He was his office clerk, he had been stealing out of the Christmas packages and Captain Hatfield told him to get his stealing ass down that hall he was not allowed back up there. I had a job change from the Shift Office to the Captains Office. I made the list up for the inmate Christmas packages.

At 10am I made 7 copies of the list one for each dorm and one for the hall bulletin board. I and Captain Hatfield & Angeles started handing out packages. You were allowed everything that was on the Christmas list up to 25 pounds. The inmate's families are very creative, they would pour out the baby oil and put in Vodka, tooth paste and lotion they would wrap drug and put down into the containers. So we had wires that we would run down into the bottles and fill to see if anything were inside. If anything was found the inmate lost the whole package and a warrant was placed on the person that sent the drugs through the United State Postal Department, it's called trafficking. This was the same routine every day until January when the package cutoff date.

1989

Now that my job title has changed my duties changed. I was up every morning at 4am. I could leave my dorm anytime I wanted to and go to the Captains office. I had keys to open the doors. My routine was up at 4am, shower, eat, go to the office and get the transfers for the day. Wake up the inmates on transfer and send them to segregation to be shaken down for transfer. Get the coffee made for the Captains, do any typing that was needed and wait for the Captains to come in to see if they needed anything.

Captain Hatfield retired this year and Captain Angeles was the Chief Captain now. They opened Loxley Road Prison up where they transferred some of the officers and the prison was short handed. So Officer Clinner was placed into the I.C.S. office which now adjoined the Captains office. She and I became best of friends, her husband worked there as the accounting office supervisor.

Now my duties went a step higher. I had to do all the typing for the Captain, Bed assignments, Job assignments, Transfers, Count board, any typing that had to be done, go to the farm gate and school gate and help with checkouts. This went from 4am until after 5pm everyday but weekends and Holidays. I had keys to places that some officers couldn't go. That's when I got the nick name the little Warden. I basically ran the prison from the inside. Even Officers would come to me for transfers and raises; I would have to type the officer's evaluations. I could sign Captain Angeles name better than he could. And yes, I got his approval.

The trade school was coming out with a new class called computer technology and accounting, I wanted to get my degree in that area. I went to Captain Angeles and ask if I could go to trade school and take the class. This was my answer, "You can go as long as your work is done each day in the office." So, I would have to get up eat, go to the office and do all my transfers, and get the checkout cards for the farm and trade school ready, assign beds for the new inmates coming in on transfer. Then get the 6am count ready, as soon as the count was cleared head to the farm gate for checkout, then go checkout the trade school, I would be the last inmate thought the gate. I would go to class. Come back into the camp for lunch. Go to the office pull the afternoon stop-ups, and any typing that was needed. At 1pm head to the farm checkout gate and then to the trade school. At 4pm I would come into the camp ahead of everyone and eat my supper, and head to the office. I would have to do all the inmate population bed changes, job changes, and any typing that was needed, plus type the daily bulletin. Get the count board straightened out so I could wash and repeat the next day.

While walking down the hall one day I saw a guard go flying from the chow hall door to the wall in the hall, then I saw another. I run to the Captains office and told Captain Angeles what was going on, He told me to go back and see what was happening. When I got there an inmate was grabbing officers with one hand and throwing them out of the chow hall. I went back and told the Captain what I saw. He told me to go and stop it. So, I went and ask one of the officers why the inmate was going crazy, he did not really know. So I found out the inmate was inmate Asbill, so I went into the chow hall waited for inmate Asbill to set down at his table and I got on the other side from him. I ask him why were the officers trying to fight him. He said, "A preacher came to his table and was bothering him while he was eating and he ask him to leave, when he didn't he slapped him away from the table." I said ok, I'll be back when you're done eating. I went to the office and told Captain what he said and who it was. Captain wanted to know if Asbill had taken his medication today, I didn't know. I went back and ask Asbill had he been to the infirmary, he said No. Well, told him he needed to go take his medication. He said No, because when he walked out of the chow hall the officers would jump him and beat him up. So, I made him a promise, I told him I would walk him to the infirmary and if he saw an officer on the hall he could beat me, He agreed. So I walk outside the chow hall and told the officers the deal and if I saw a blue suite on the hall and they get me beat I was coming for them and transfer them to a prison they would not like. I went back into the chow hall got Asbill and took him to the infirmary to get his medication, and then I took him back to his dorm and put him to bed. Asbill was on some wild medication called Thorazine, it calms the gentle giants.

OK, this is how the trade school was set-up and all the things they offered. You have to be checked out and counted. The trade school yard was fenced in like the prison with 4 gun towers. Normally Officer Haney was at the tower by the shake down shack, and Officer C. Hall was at the front tower where the entrance gate was. The trade school was made up of GED classed, Culinary, Computer Technology & Accounting, Cabinet making & wood work, Cosmetology, Shoe & Boot making and repair, Small engine repair, Welding, Auto Body repair, and Auto repair. If you had a long sentence you could receive a degree in all the classes offered.

When you come back into the prison you have to go through a shakedown shack, Farm or trade school. This means you have to get as naked as you were when you were born. You open your mouth, lift up your dick & nut sack, and bend over and spread your butt cheeks. Walk into the other side of the room put your clothes back on and go into the camp. You are counted each time to make sure the count matched when you checked out. If the count does not match, this meant that we go into lock down. The Dog Wardens were called so they could have the dogs to search the buildings and fences. I have to go to the office and make copies of the bed rooster so we can do a bed check to see who is missing. If the count is messed up from the trade school count all eyes are on the trade school grounds. The guards would have to search each building.

One day while helping check trade school back in, I was standing on the prison side of the shack down shack. All of a sudden someone come running through the shack, and the officers yelled catch him. So I ran him down and bull dogged him behind Dorn #2. When I caught him it was inmate John (AKA) Buckshot. He pleaded with me to take him to the infirmary, so I took him to the Hospital. When we got there they found a Suave Shampoo bottle in his butt. He had put mineral spirits in it to bring back into the camp to sale in the hobby shop. Well it had sprung a leak and was setting his guts and tell hole on fire. The doctor fished it out and he went to lockup.

We did have three inmates take a car and run it through the fence of the trade school. They didn't get very far; the car had bullet holes everywhere. Sgt. W. Hall took his truck and run the car off the road along with the Dog Wardens and brought them back to the prison. Needless to say after that point all drive shafts were taken out of all vehicles brought into the trade school for work to be done on them.

One day while out at the trade school two guys got into a fight over a punk. Both of them wanted him so they got into a fight to try and prove who he would be with. Well with the welding shop being out there they had made some fine knives. One of the guys got stabbed in the side of his neck and I was close by. It had cut the artery in his neck blood was going everywhere. I grabbed him and stuck my fingers into his neck to stop the blooding. Officer C. Hall had me to bring him to the gate, they had the dog truck there and we put him up on the dog box. When we went by the front of the prison they stopped for one of the nurses to get on the truck with us. We rode all the way to Atmore hospital on the back of the dog truck with sirens on and blue lights flashing. I was covered in blood, but the boy lived. He stayed in the hospital for about a week. When he came down the hall he came and thanked me for helping save his life. When he got better and his neck movement back I made him thank me in a better way. Yea, I'm bad.

Since I brought up the Dog Wardens let me tell you a little of their jobs and who they were at the time. Warden Knowles, Warden Townsend, and Warden Mustin. Their job at the prison was to train dogs to track escaped inmates. Sometimes the county and highway patrol would use them to catch people that run from cars or houses. Understand this was before a lot of towns had patrol dogs. The Wardens had to keep up with four prisons, Fountain Correctional Facility, J.O. Davis Corrections Center, Atmore Work Release, and Holman Correctional Facility. They had one dog that was trained for drugs. Warden Mustin was his handler, and I got to keep him in my office when he came down the hall.

To tell you a little bit about the Computer class I was in. We were taught how to write computer programs and accounting. The computers were on the Basic DOS systems, binary code where we had to learn to read ones and zeros to make a program (111000010010000101) do you know what I just wrote? Something for you to think of. Then we were taught the basics of accounting on balancing books, debits, credits, and assets. I was busier than a one arm wallpaper hanger. But I designed a program off the Q&A system that cut my work load in half. Understand computers had not been introduced into the Alabama prison system; everything was done by type writer and copy machine. With this system I could put the inmates name and information into the computer when they arrived at Fountain. The system would alphabetize the names and put the beds in numerical order. NO more typing a 1,200 name alpha list and bed rooster once a week, the computer would do it automatically. Life was turned easy for me. Captain Angeles, said that the class has paid off for me and the prison system. Fountain was built to house 888 inmates, but was holding 1,266 at the time. Each dorm down the hall was different. Dorms #1, #2, #3, #4 had 200 beds in each; Dorms #5 and #6 had 35 beds each. 63 beds in the portable trailers. Segregation had four sides with 40 single man beds on each block. Then the Infirmary had 15 beds for sick inmates.

1990

ell another year has come and gone. And I now have my custody, this means I can go outside of the fence without an officer with me. So I talked to Captain Angeles to see if I could go work with the horses when I had some spare time. He agreed, so when school was out and I was not really busy in the office I would check myself out and go ride the horses, I just had to be back to the prison by dark. One day when we had No school and I was not busy in the office, I helped with checkout and then when to the barn and saddled up a horse. The farm guards were on their horses with their squad of inmate work. I would ride be and see what was going on. I heard Officer Dawson come over the radio and ask Sgt. W. Hall to come relieve him because he had to use the bathroom. No one answered his call, so he called again. Still no one answered and he stood up in the saddle and shit down both of his pant legs. That's where Officer Dawson got the nick name Shitty leg Dawson. Apparently Officer Dawson had been stealing the other officer's deserts, so they made him a present with Ex-lax. That's one way to stop a thief.

I took my horse and would ride all over the state property from Fountain to Holman. I got to where I knew the property like the back of my hand. I was talking to Dog Warden Mustin one day and ask him could I help train the dogs. Well, they already had inmates from J.O. Davis Correctional Facility to run what they called shams, that where the Dog Warden would take the inmate and drop them where they wanted to start the dogs for training and tell them where to stop. They would walk or run thought the woods and try to trick the dogs so they could not catch them. Sometimes they would wait 30 minutes before they let the dogs lose up to 3 hours. Then follow the dogs to see if they could find them. Fountain held the 4A state dog championship for having so well trained dogs. So, one day Dog Warden Mustin allowed me to run a sham. I tried all the tricks they talk about on T.V. how to shake dogs. As soon as I got to water I went up stream for about 100 yards then climbed a tree and went from one tree to the other because they were so close. When I arrived to the area I was suppose to wait for the dogs at I climbed a tree and waited. Well you need to tell the T.V. people they don't know what they are talking about, water only helps a dog not to burn out and it enhances your smell and keeps it fresh. The dogs found me within 2 hours after I was let out to start my trail. They had let loose 5 dogs 3 beagles and 2 hounds one was a red bone and the other was a bloodhound and red bone mix. The hound that was mixed was named Hudo, this dog would get faster the deeper in the water you got into, and he loved it. I would help train off and on because Dog Wardens Knowles & Townsend like the way I tried to trick the dogs. It just made them smarter.

The Amish and Mennonites come to the prison and spend a full week visiting with inmates at their dorms and beds. A family called the Wissmann family came to the prison and sang and played their instruments. One of their sons out of 13 kids played the steel guitar. He really made the show. The others in the family played guitars, fiddles, Mandolin, the upright bass, and sang.

I know I have not said much about visits. But, my mother and my friend Eleanor would come to visit me most every weekend. We would set out on the visiting yard, talk and eat. Captain Angeles made good friends with my mother and Eleanor. So on my birthday those two got together and mailed a package to me at the prison in care of Captain Angeles. When Mr. Reynolds the mailman got it he called me to pick up the package for Captain Angeles, when I got it to the office Captain Angeles told me to open it because my name was on it. Well, when I go it open there was a full beef side of cooked ribs. Those two had talk and wanted me to have ribs for my birthday. So I took them to the chow hall and got the Stewart to warn them in the oven. I took them back to the Captains office and we pigged out, Angeles, Clinner, and two other inmates. Yummy! First Ribs I have had in 4 years.

I had made friends with an inmate that worked in maintenance inmate Stewart. This man had a hell of a story why he was in prison; my opinion is he should not be there. I was walking across the yard going to the back gate and saw him walking across the yard with a lawnmower blade in his hand. I approached him and ask him where he was going with the blade. He said, "He was going to kill inmate Billy." I ask why? He said, "Billy was talking about hurting me and he was going to kill him before he could." I told him I would not let him do that, he already had a life sentence and I was not going to let him do something to jeopardize his freedom for me. So I set on his feet and rapped my arms around his legs and ask him would he hurt me. He said, "NO." So, I ask him to give me the blade. I looked like a nut setting on a man's feet out in the middle of a yard. I finally got him to give me the blade and we both walked back to the maintenance building.

Well I had a new boyfriend, this son of a bitch looked like Mister Olympia, and he worked out on the weight pile most every day. He was inmate Herrin, that boy could eat ass, suck and fuck like know one's business. He and I would shower and go back to my bed where I would give him a massage and he would eat my ass and suck my dick. One day we were talking and he ask me for a transfer to Ventress Correctional Facility, they would let him out early if he took the classes there. I told him No, and when I did he slapped me. He said, "Now lock me up and transfer me." I said No, I told him to never put his hands on me ever again.

I waited about a week and walked out to the weight pile while he was working out, picked up a 2.5 pound weight and he was dead lifting over 500 pounds, once he locked his arms in I hit him right between the eyes. He dropped the weights on his cheat and broke a lot of bones. I told him if he lived he would learn to never put his hands on me every again. The Officers came and got him and carried him to the infirmary.

I went back to the office and Captain Angeles come in and said, "Why are you trying to kill your man?" I told him what Herrin had done a few weeks ago and I was teaching him a listen. He said, "You damn near killed him, so I am locking him in segregation when the hospital releases him for his safety." Well Herrin stayed in the hospital for a week and in segregation for two weeks when I went up to see him. When I walked into the segregation unit I went to his cell and ask him has he learned his listen about slapping me. He said, "You almost killed me." I told him if he every raised his hand to me again I would. I told him to pack his shit that the next morning he was on transfer to Ventress.

Well after Herrin was transferred I started hanging out with one of his best fiends inmate Wilkins, he was built too. But he didn't know how to do what Herrin could. He had his custody and Dog Warden need some trails cut in the woods and some snakes killed. Well he was the guy for the job, when he was on the streets he handled snakes so he loved catching them. So we went to the woods and cut trails and he dove into the water after the mother cottonmouth snake, I killed the babies. About 30 minutes later I heard him yelling. I went to whcrc he was and he said he could not get through the brayers and fight that big ass snake. He has swum he creek until he caught the snake. I cut the brayers out of the way so he could get out of water. He needed the area clear so he could put it on the ground and played with it for a while before we killed it and moved on. We stopped to rest and I pulled his pants off to suck his dick and there was the littlest dick I have ever seen on a grown man. If it was big as my finger on hard I was exaggerating.

I had been fucking inmate Glover most every morning when I showered getting ready for work. He was the runner on the night shift in the shift commander office. He started doing it out of the blue; I was not expecting it to happen. Standing there showering and he dropped him wash cloth on the shower floor in front of me, when he bent over to pick it up he started sucking my dick. Once he got it hard he bent over and took it like a man. And that happened a lot over the next year or so.

One day I when down to Dorm #2 to find an inmate that the Captain wanted to see. I opened the door and walked in yelled the inmates name and started talking to Officer McCadden who was in the cell. Inmate Bullard walked up to me and slapped me on the neck, when he did by reflex I grabbed Officer McCaddens knight stick and hit him with it. Bullard started trying to run away from me and I knocked him to the floor and started beating his head into the concrete. Office McCadden told me to get off him, I told him the bitch slapped me and I was going to stop him from slapping people. Officer McCadden said, "No he didn't he cut your throat." I looked down and blood was all over my shirt. So I beat his head into the concrete a few more time before Officer McCadden pulled me off. I got up and went back to the office. I went into the bathroom and tried to clean up; Captain Angeles wanted to know if I was ok. I said I was find I had a little cut. He walked in and looked and said,"Damn, someone has tied to cut your fucking head off. Get your ass to the infirmary." I walked out to the infirmary and the nurses started panicking saying I needed stitched and I needed to go to Atmore hospital. I said oh hell no I'm not going to the hospital and went to the back and started cleaning up the cut. I told the nurses they needed to help the bastard that was come I beat the hell out of. I got some alcohol and triple antibiotic, got it clean put some butterfly strips on it and a 4x4 bandage over it. I walked out and they were working on inmate Bullard. When I got to the office Captain Angeles said I needed to go relax and change clothing. I said No I'm going to walk around and let the population see what inmate Bullard did and where he is now and I'm not scared of any of them.

Captain Angeles and I were setting in the office talking and working. One of the officers brought in two 5 gallon buckets full of Julip; it was made with Donald Duck Orange juice. Captain Angeles said bring me a cup and sampled the julip. He told me I should try some because it was good. I said I'll pass because I don't drink Alcohol. I had to go find a glass jug and bottle up the stuff; Captain Angeles wanted to take it home.

They decided to build a new dorm, and it didn't take too long, just a metal building. After it was built they transferred some of Holman's inmates to stay in the dorm while they built one over at Holman. I was walking down the hall to the shift office and I saw a fight on the yard. I saw one inmate stab the other inmate, I yelled Lock this son of a bitch down and bring me a gurney. When I got to the guy it was inmate Russell, I saw his eyes roll back in his head, he made two steps and fell, and his head hit the sidewalk. He was dead when he hit the sidewalk. The officers locked the yard down and we got Inmate Russell to the infirmary where they said he was dead something I already knew. Inmate Russell was killed because he had let the other inmate wear his gold neck less our on the visiting yard and gave it to his girlfriend. When he came back down the hall inmate Russell wanted his neck less back and the other inmate told him to kick rocks he gave it to his girl. That's when the fight broke out.

When the inmates from Holman had been there for a few weeks they tried to start a riot. They held Officer Fequa hostage in Dorm #7. We also got a new Captain Ferrell he was over the SWAT team. We locked the side yard down so they could not come into the main camp to fight. We had a big meeting in the office. I told Captain Angeles that we should put Captain Ferrell into a set of whites to look like an inmate since no one knew him and he could go with me to Dorm #7. Once we get into the dorm we could get officer Fegua and get him out. Well this is how it went. We went into the dorm and they had Officer Fequa in the cub in the center of the dorm, I told Captain Ferrell since he was bigger than me to grab Officer Fequa, I would take a fire extinguisher and fog the room behind us so the inmates would stay back. So the plan came together and we got Officer Fequa out. I yelled to the guards on the fiancé to shoot and kill anyone that come out of the dorm. We took Officer Fequa to the infirmary to treat his injuries, while there he told us the inmate's names that started the riot. Captain Ferrell took his SWAT team out there and took the dorm back over and got the inmates that were causing problems and locked them in the segregation unit. When it was all said and done Captain Ferrell was in the office talking with Captain Angeles and me and wanted to know how an inmate had so much power. Captain Angeles told him my history. Now he understands why I was called the little warden.

There was an inmate who everyone called preacher Henry. He was always quoting scripture to the inmates. While I was in the shower one afternoon after work he came into the bathroom and the next thing I knew he had snuck into the shower with me sucking my dick. This sucker was no normal dick sucker; he could take 9.5 inches down his throat with no problem and wanted more. He wanted me to cum down his throat. This guy had no gag reflex, Hallelujah brother.

1991

Things in prison are basically the same every day, everyone has a routine, Holiday's and weekends are the only things that are different, and then you have Christmas every year. Since I set up the computer system the prison decided to have an incentive package program. If you have a 6 month clear record with no disciplinarians and citations you could receive a package every three months. This gave the inmate population the incentive to not misbehave. So I set up a program to show which inmates were eligible.

Understand prisons are like a small city inside a fence. It has a store so you can inmates can catch store once a week, there's a post office, barber shop, music department, sports department, infirmary, and business office. As Assistant Warden Ross would say you act crazy and want to fight they have a place to put you so you can be controlled they even have a jail.

With me being the little warden I could sleep where ever I wanted to sleep. My Bed assignment was Dorm#5 bed#13; my bed was right under a fan since prisons have NO air conditioning other than the offices. My friends that was in my dorm, was a serial killer, a grand old man inmate Monroe. I would set and talk to him and he had some stories. I loved to hear about what made him tick. Then I had the great inmate Stewart who worked maintenance, Boy I wish I could tell you his store why he was in there for NO reason. Remember the inmate throwing the Officers out of the chow hall inmate Asbill? Inmate Bullock who raped the Delchamp grocery chain daughter. There was an inmate we called Mac Nasty, Ash. Inmate Doppie, Landry, guess how he got his nick name? And you had inmate Gill, he was the computer whiz kid.

I would go out to dorm #7 and hook up with a guy name William he was kind of nice to have sex with. I also had inmate Robbin still who worked on radios for other inmates. One night I gave my key to the law library to an inmate I thought I could trust and had him to lock me and Robbin in there so we could have sex. While we were having sex Officer Gandy and Hatcher came into the library to catch us, we hide under the desk but they found us. Officer Hatcher has never liked me because he thought an inmate should not have as much authority that I had. So he tried to have me and Robbin locked into segregation, that didn't work because Lt. Williams wanted to know what the charge was? Officer Hatcher said attempted escape. Lt. Williams said, we were not trying to get out of the prison. So he couldn't have us locked up. Officer Hatcher was mad, so he still tried to write us both disciplinaries. When I got to the office the next day I put Officer Hatcher in for a transfer to Loxley prison. The disciplinaries were lost in the paper shuffle.

One day while out riding my horse I stopped next to the road and tied my horse in the woods. Yes I left him with food and water. My mother came and picked me up to go into Atmore and eat at Dave's catfish house. I had a change of clothing in the car. No I did not have permission to go off prison property. While I was there eating I looked up and saw Captain Angeles, Lt. Thomas, Warden Holt and some other people coming in to eat. I dipped down below the table so I would not be seen. I met mother out at the car while she paid the bill. She took me back to where my horse was at; I changed back into my prison clothing. I went back to the camp and checked in. Everything was good, Captain Angeles came back to the office and I was doing my work. About the time Captain Angeles started to leave for the day he said as he started out the door, "I hope you enjoyed your fish dinner today." It was never mentioned anymore. But I never pushed my luck like that anymore.

This was a very sad time in my life. I was notified that my heart and soul had died Mickey my first true love. His mother said he had a bad liver condition and the doctors did not have anything to help him so he died from it. My heart has been broken ever since. Yes I have had sex with a lot of people but he was my heart and there is a void in my soul.

One of the inmates Allen worked in the small engine repair shop. Everyone was always pulling pranks on him, but he was also pulling pranks on people as well. His job was to test all the engines before they left the yard to assure they worked. Well they had a go-cart that had to be tested. The guys in the shop had fixed the accelerator to stick wide open and unhooked the brakes, Well when Allen got on the go-cart to test drive it, he started around the yard and he was wide open coming through and trying to stand up on the brakes that didn't work. He would reach back to unplug the spark plug and it was shock him, he would come past us yelling woo Ouch Ouch!!! It was funny while it lasted, but he lost control of it and went under the razor wire. Everyone run over to help try and get him out, his legs got cut up but he was Ok. A few days we all set around and laughed about, because it was funny to see it.

November the 21th I graduated my Computer Technology and Accounting class. I have now gotten my diploma saying I am officially a Computer Technologists and Accountant. We had a big graduation party and the Alabama prison is now one step higher in technology.

While at Fountain I had had sex with, Robbin, Breeden, Herrin, Herny, Glover, William, Reliford, Gill, James, Wilkins, Russell, Barrett, and a few others I can't remember their names.

1992

I remain working in the Captains office and going out to play with the horses. Captain Angeles had me to set down one day in the office and we had a long talk. He told me that he thinks it is time for me to go home and I needed to start making the steps to get there. He thought it was a good idea for me to transfer to J.O. Davis trustee camp right behind Fountain. So I agreed to the transfer. So in (6) six weeks I was transferred to J.O. Davis trustee camp.

I went to work for the tractor shop as their accountant. I had my own office up stairs overlooking the shop. I think I had sex with every tractor driver we had on the crew. I would even go out to the gas pump shed and have sex in the shed with the guy Robert that ran the pumps. This was going to be a fun job. One of the guys that was on the tractor crew come up to my office one morning and wanted to have sex, while he was there they called him because he was being released from prison early, but he didn't leave my office until he was finished having sex. LOL!! This went on for a few months, and the dog warden requested me to be transferred to the dog team.

Well now my new assignment Saddle house and Dog tracking team. I would train horses for the guards to ride and take the inmate squads out. I would also train the tracking dogs how to track escaped inmates and people that were running from law enforcement. Our dog Wardens were Captain Knowels. Captain Townsend and Captain Mustin. I trained dogs that won the State's 3A dog tracking Championship.

I would get woken up many times at night to make dog runs; we would take the dogs to track down people running from law enforcement. I would run with the dogs sometimes or ride on the horses to keep up with the dogs, it would vary. One time that sticks in my head was. Two guys had killed there school teacher for turning them in for stealing a four wheeler. One of the guys was an inmate that had been at Fountain named John. We were all on horseback and the dogs had bayed the two guys down in a swampy area. I got off my horse and walked down where they were at, Captain Knowles and Townsend waited for me to get back with the dogs. I called John. (Aka) Buckshot (yes, the same guy that had the bottle up his ass I took to the hospital in 1989) and told him I was only coming in to get the dogs and they needed to give up. Buckshot said they had a .22 rifle and they were not going back to prison. I walked out with the dogs and told Captain Knowles and Townsend where they were and that they were armed. They grabbed their shotguns and walked down in to the edge of the swamp and told them to give up. Buckshot said they were not coming out, if they wanted to get it on. Captain Knowles said then let's get it on, and started shooting. They had a pretty good gun fight. Buckshot got hit and started yelling to stop. I walked back down into the area where they were at and found the both of them shot up pretty good. I took my horse and rope and tied the rope around them and drug them out to the road so the ambulance could get to them. Otherwise, they would have probably died down in the swamp. Buckshot lost one of his legs from gunshot and one of his nuts, but he is alive and still doing time at Holman prison.

While I was there the Warden over J.O. Davis and I bumped heads. I don't remember his name because he told me, if I didn't like the way he ran J.O. Davis I could go back to Fountain. I was so use to running Fountain he didn't like the way I thought J.O. Davis should be ran. He didn't last long because I called the commissioner (Thigpin) and they moved him. I guess he found out how much power I still had.

I trained dogs and horses for the dog team for 2 years, and there are a lot of stories that can be told. Like where all the dead bodies are buried that surpassingly escaped years ago. Yes, I found where a lot of bodies are buried. I actually fell into one of the old graves while out training dogs, that was one of the times in my life I really got spooked. But, I was told to never speak of it. But, I still know the spot and place to this day no matter how the woods may have changed I still know where that spot is.

I could write a book on all the stories in detail of the people that we chased and inmates we caught while on the dog team. But if this book goes well I will come back and write stories of things that happened in detail. Like inmates eating mushrooms and spacing out escaping.

I told you while I was at Fountain about Asbill and Stewart; well they came to J.O. Davis with me. Asbill and I would sit outside a lot. There was a clover patch he loved to lay in and look for 4 leaf clovers, and at night he would stare into the stars talking about the satellites' and different things in outer space. Asbill could tell you the difference between a star and satellite, plus the different plains that would fly over. He was an amazing and smart man.

Stewart was the head maintenance man at J.O. Davis and he tapped into the gas lines in the kitchen and he made us an outside gas grill. I would catch rabbits, snakes, raccoon, and every now and then kill a deer. Boy would we have a cook out. Some of the inmates that were jealous told on him because they had to eat the nasty food out of the chow hall and we were eating high on the deer or ever what else we could catch or kill to cook.

One day while at the saddle house one of the horses becomes sick. The inmates at J.O. Davis had been feeding them bread over the fence and it caused the horse to get what we call foundered. That means he could not crap. So I took him to the barn and got a water hose and was putting the hose up the horses butt when another inmate come into the barn and started asking questions. He was standing behind the horse as I was putting water in the horses butt. He kept asking what you are doing. What are you doing? I told him he better move and he kept standing behind the horse, asking what you are doing. When I pulled the water hose out of the horses butt shit covered him. I said that's what I'm doing, the horse couldn't shit; now he's cleaned out and won't be sick anymore. Dumbass city boys get to learn how to doctor horses with shit all over them. You had to be there, it was so funny.

1993

*W*ell this year I was allowed to start taking passes. This is where your family members can come get you for 8 hours and go eat or anything else you want to do. Even though I had already been going to eat and do things with my mother, I'm doing it legal now. One of my times I remember well was my mother and Uncle Woody came to get me and we went fishing at a damn just north of Atmore. We were in my uncles new red truck, we were going through the woods to get to the place he wanted to show us and we went around a sharp curb and he said, "That curb was so sharp that the mule could eat the corn out the back of the wagon it was so sharp." I almost wet my paints laughing, yes I know it's corny but I thought it was funny. One if my great times with my mother and uncle before he died. About 3 months later I was called to the front office and told to call my mother it was an emergency. When I called mother told me that uncle Woody had died of a massive heart attack.

While at J.O. Davis I had sex with 4 guys in the saddle house. Two guys that was on the tractor crew, the guy that run the gas house, and a few guys that were in the camp. Plus one really wild experience in one of the mop closets.

In October I was transferred to Atmore Work Release, right across the field. The Warden was Mr. Weaver, quite a guy. He put me to work with the lady who ran the accounting office for the work release, Ms. Odan, very sweat lady. I was posting the inmate money that was received and counting out money for the inmate pay roll each week.

I had to help working in the kitchen for a little while. The head Stewart Mr. Reynolds left me over the kitchen one weekend and we were having Hamburgers and French fries. While I was cooking the French fries a inmate came into the back that didn't work in the kitchen trying to tell me how to cook, said that I should not put salt on fries when they come out of the hot grease. I just so happened to keep a big knife in the back of my pants to open the packs of fries, and you got it; I pulled it and run his ass out of the kitchen. Officer Folks, she told me that I couldn't be doing things like that they would transfer me back to Fountain. I told her they couldn't put me No place I have never been. If she didn't want me to do those kinds of things to keep inmates out of the kitchen that were not suppose to be in it.

Well when Warden Weaver came back that Monday he called me into his office and told me he would have probably done the something, but these officers didn't like what I did so he said he was going to take me out of the kitchen, so I would not get into trouble. So he sent me to the Evergreen Highway patrol station. Every morning officer Gore would come pick me up and we would go to the Highway Patrol station, I would clean the offices and mow the grass. Once I was done with everything I would set with the Dispatcher and answer the phone and dispatch patrol cars. This went on for a few months and one day there was a very bad accident, Officer Gore called into the office and said he would not be able to take me back to the camp for me to take the spare patrol car and go back to camp. So I got the keys and went back to the camp, I gave the officers at the camp the keys to the patrol car. They didn't like that I was driving a patrol car. The next morning I got ready and went to the cube and told the officer that I needed the key to the patrol car so I could go back to work. While driving up interstate 65 a car was driving 60 in the fast lane and I pulled in behind him because he was backing up traffic, I flipped in the blue lights and siren, he drove his car into the median of the highway, and I didn't slow down until I got to the patrol office.

William

While I was at the work release I hooked up with two guys James and William. Even though these two guys had girlfriends on the street they were still fun to have sex with. When William was released he moved out to California and stayed in contact with me for a few years.

Every weekend I was going on passes with mother to have fun. Well Christmas rolled around and I was eligible for a 3 day furlough. I ask Warden Weaver could I go home for Christmas. He said put it on paper and he would sign it. Well Christmas rolled around and mother came to pick me up, I stayed the night and woke up to Christmas. We opening up our Christmas packages and the phone rang. It was Officer Folks from the Work Release, She said, "Is this Lonnie, I said yes, she said I was in violation of the rules and in an unauthorized area and if I didn't return to the camp I would be charged with escape. So mother started crying, she had just had surgery and was not filling good. So my step father Dan took me back to the camp and gave them a few choice words for screwing his wife's Christmas. Well, they had me to pack my things up and send them home with Dan, then sent me back to Fountain in lock up.

Well, the next morning while in lock up I was woken up to the voice of Captain Angeles. He said, "Get your ass up! What happened?" Well I got up and told him what had taken place. He said, here's your keys back, go down the hall and find me a bed. So, I went down the hall and got me a bed, and Monday morning I was in the office with coffee made for everyone. Captain Angeles called Warden Weaver and they talked. Then Captain Angeles told me to go up front and talk to the legal officer Mr. Thomas and tell him what had taken place. Well officer Thomas and I had a long talk, he wanted to see my paperwork where Warden Weaver signed my 3 day furlough, and he told me not to worry about anything.

Well officer Folks served me with a disciplinary for being in an unauthorized area for my furlough; I had two weeks to prepare my case.

e went to disciplinary court and I had several questions for officer Folks.

1). Officers Folks, Was inmate Marshall at the place Warden Weaver had signed his furlough to be at? Her answer, Yes

2). Officer Folks, Did you talk to inmate Marshall at the phone number on his 3 day furlough? Her answer, Yes

3). Officer Folks, Did inmate Marshall come back the Work Release when you instructed him to? Her answer, Yes

After these questions officer Thomas asked Officer Folks how inmate Marshall can be found guilty for being in an unauthorized area when a DOC official signed the paperwork where he was at when you talked to him. Inmate Marshall was where a DOC official told him he could be at, and after you called inmate Marshall and told him to return to the camp he returned in a timely manner, so therefore he did as he was told. This case is dismissed. Inmate Marshall you're not guilty of your charges.

I got up from the hearing and shook officers Thomas's hand, Officer Folks stormed out of the room. Officer Thomas said, "You have worked at this prison and helped a great deal. You might not want to go back to Atmore Work Release because she will be gunning for you. Go to a different Work Center, and go home." I told him thanks once again and left out of the room and went back to the Captains office to work. Captain Angeles ask how it went. I told him what had taken place, and Officer Thomas said don't go back to

Atmore Work Release because she would be gunning for me to screw up. Captain Angeles said put yourself in for a transfer to Montgomery Work Center. So I did and I was gone in two weeks.

While I was waiting to leave in those two weeks I had sex with inmate James, Williams, and Jerry. Inmate Jerry was almost as fine as Herrin, Damn he was fun. He and I also met and hooked up after we were released from prison.

On arrival at Montgomery Work Center I was told I would be assigned to the kitchen for a few weeks and start work on a job. I did my tour in the kitchen and received a job as an Accountant and Payroll clerk with Buckhannon Construction Company. There I met Mr. Mimms the head mechanic. Mimms was a great guy; I would get all my work caught up and go outside and help him in the shop. I would wear my cowboy hat at work and he would play games on me all the time taking my hat and putting it on piles outside and other places. Well I was normally the first person to get to the office everyday and I went into the shop and filled his tool box with oil and took a chain hoist to the top of the rafters in the shop and pulled the tool box to the top. When Mimms got to work he said for me to call the police someone had took all his tools. I told him he might want to look around like I have to looking for my hat before he calls the police. After an hour he finally found his tool box in the top of the shop. He started laughing and said how did you get that damn thing up there? I said the same way you're going to get it down.

After several months working there a company called Church and Tower bought Buckhannon Construction Company, a guy named Mas bought it come to the shop, he had his two sons' with him. As time went on we made a great rapport with each other. I was told every time Mr. Mas come to town I was to be beside his side. I would meet him at the Air Port and he would always ride with me in the company truck.

He gave me a bulletproof vest and gun a told me to wear it when we were out with each, I might have to save his life some day. I told him you know I'm not supposed to have a gun because of being in prison. He said don't worry he had my back. So sure enough, one day while we were out a person come up be hide us with a shotgun and I grabbed Mr. Mas when the person shot. I took the full hit in my vest, and fell on Mr. Mas. When I rolled over I shot the guy right in the head. When Mr. Mas got through talking to the police nothing was ever said.

I remember one morning Mr. Mas called me and told me to meet him at the Air Port early in the morning. When his plane landed he told me to get in to the plane. I told him I couldn't because I had to be back at the prison at night. He said he would have me back in time to be at the prison. We flow to Tampa, Florida to the home he had down there and he showed me where he lived. We talked about all his businesses in Florida, Alabama, and Georgia. He told me about him being a political prisoner in Cuba and would be the next president of Cuba if Castro were to die. He said since I saved his life I was part of his family, and he would always be in debt to me. He made sure that I was flown back so I could get back to the prison on time.

I served my time at the Montgomery Work Center and worked at the Church and Tower Company. It had came time for me to go up for Parole. I was taken to meet the Alabama Attorney General Mr. Evans by Mr. Mas, He heard my story of why I was in prison and what I have done while in prison. Mr. Evans told me to take my 3 day furlough the week I go up for parole; he said he would see me there.

Sure thing I took my 3 day furlough and went to my parole hearing, my mother, Sister Pat, and I were at the hearing. They called us into the hearing room; there were 4 people on this high bench like they were judges looking down over us. The head person over the Board said, we are here to discuss the parole of Ronnie

Marshall. And we have here today Mrs. Hix his mother, Pat his sister and we have something very unusual Mr. Marshall himself. They ask me if I would like to stand and speak on my behalf, I said I would love to. I got up and walked to the stand where there was a microphone. I started talking and said, "I started doing my sentence in 1986 and while being in the system I introduced the first computer system into the prison system, I worked as the Captains clerk for 5 years, I saved a officer from being killed in a riot, I trained tracking dogs for the prison system and won the 3 A tracking team for 3 years in a row, I had received a education in computer Technology & Accounting, and I am now at Montgomery Work Center working." The head hearing person said, you can stop talk now we are going to grant you your parole. My mother jumped to her feet and yelled hallelujah Thank you Jesus!!! I walked up and shook all the members' hands and started out the door, I still had not saw Mr. Evans. We got outside the parole office and Mr. Evans walked up and asked how did it go? I said they granted my parole, where were you? He said I had already spoken to them and it would not look good if I was in the room while they made their decision. I said I understand and thank you very much for your help. We all left and went to get something to eat.

This all took place in October and it would take a few months for the paperwork to go through. They had to contact Florida and do an international compact for me to be transferred to my home in Florida.

CHAPTER 4

1995

Well the New Year came and went; I continued working at Church and Tower while at the Montgomery Work Center. I was trying to stay busy while waiting on the paperwork to be done for my release to go home.

Mean while at the Office we had this older black man Mr. Smith who was always the last one to get to the office and I had to wait for all the trucks to come in so I could lock the office and gates. I told Mimms that we needed to do something about this because I would like to leave before dark. So I had finished my work in the office and went out driving my company truck and saw a raccoon get hit by a car. I stopped my truck and put the dead raccoon in the back of my truck. When I got back to the office I took a string and tied it around the raccoon's neck and went to Mr. Smith's truck. I tied the other end of the string to the driver's door and laid the raccoon in the passenger seat. When Mr. Smith opens his door it will look like the raccoon is coming after him.

Just like clockwork at dark Mr. Smith come driving up into the company yard to put up his truck. I went out and locked the gates. Mr. Smith went out to get into his truck to go home. When he opened the door the dome light come on and all he saw was a raccoon coming across the truck seat toward him. Yes he screamed really loud. LOL!!! I walked out and told him next time it could be a live raccoon or snake, start getting into the yard before dark. He was always into the yard before it got dark from that day forward.

Finally in March I got word that I would be released on the next Monday. I called my mother and told her to come and get me the next Monday. When I got up that Monday morning, I went over into the Montgomery Work Center office I had to sign all my paperwork so I could be released. I walked out to my mother's car and we left and went to the Church and Tower office where I could get all my things from there and say bye to everyone. I called Mr. Mas and told him I was leaving, He said I always have a place if I ever needed a job or anything. Then we headed to Pensacola, Florida.

I stayed with my mother and worked as an accountant with a Farm & nursery Mart. I had saved up $10,000 while in work release I had enough money to buy myself a car and look for a place to live other than with my mother.

On July 4th 1995, I met Ron at the round up Bar. I thought it was love popping all around me when the fireworks went off. I thought I had found my true love once again. We found a house to rent on New Warrington road in Pensacola where we lived for quit sometime. While at work one day at Farm & Nursery I received a phone call, it was Mama Kadenhead. She told me to come quick that she thinks Papa is dead. Well the Farm & Nursery is only less than one mile down the road. I jumped into my car and down the road I flew, when I got there I ran inside and she said he was in the bedroom. When I got back there I checked his pulse, my heart was beating so hard and fast I thought he was still alive. I started CPR, when the volunteer fireman got there he checked his pulse and said he was dead. I stayed there with Mama Kadenhead until the coroner arrived and took the body. Mama Kadenhead and I started getting funeral services ready.

Four days later we had the funeral at Pensacola NAS cemetery; this was a full military funeral. Papa Kadenhead was in World War II, Vietnam, and Korea, he was a Sergeant Major in the 82 Air Borne U.S. Army. He was highly decorated for the thing he had done while in the Army. He was buried in the Pensacola NAS Cemetery. I try to go back and visit his grave every year on Memorial Day.

I left the Nursery and went to work with Builders Ready Mix as a dispatcher and Batch man making concrete. Working with Billy who owned Builders Ready Mix was quite an experience. We would start at 2am and work unto the last truck was dispatched. I remember one of Billy and my discussions. He had asked me to do something, and it took me a while to get around to it. He ask me why it had not got done and I told him I have not had time to get to it. Billy said an excuse is nothing but a lie.

A while later a older man that worked for the company got real sick and Billy said we were going to have to have a fish fry to raise some money to pay his hospital bills. We were sitting in the church having his funeral and I ask Billy why we didn't have a fish fry to help him. Billy said I never had time to do it, I said oh an excuse which is nothing more than a lie. Billy never said anything more about excuses. LOL

(Funny story) While at Builders Ready Mix a guy that drove one of the concrete trucks had went on a vacation and come back to work telling us of his experience. George said a few months before they went on their vacation he, his wife and kids had went over to the beach and were on their way back home when he said he was going to stop at a fast food restaurant and go through the drive thru and get everyone something to eat so they would not have to cook when they got back home. Well the kids and he ordered, but his wife said, he would need to go in and get what she wanted because she didn't want her food through the drove thru. He told her that it was not happening if she wanted something to eat he would order it like he and the kids had done. She refused, so she got nothing. They started driving home and was about to get on the three mile bay bridge, she said stop the car. He stopped the car and she said she wanted out and was not riding with him. So he stopped and let her out, then drove off. Once he got to the other side of the three mile bridge he felt sorry for her and went back to get her. When he pulled up beside her he stopped and ask her to get into the car. She refused and said she was walking home. So he drove off and went home. Around 3:30am she came walking in the door dog tired. When they took their vacation to the mountains they got into another disagreement and she said stop the car I'm not riding with you! So he immediately stopped the car reached across her opened the car door for her and said, now when you get out this time remember we are in the mountains and we live on the Gulf you're going to have a little longer walk this time. She closed the door and they have not had an argument since. (True story)

Ron and I were having our problems. He was running back and forth to his old boyfriend and back to me. I finally gave him an ultimatum. So he stopped seeing his Ex as far as I know. Ron worked as a furniture salesman and when we met, He was so deep in debt he had no credit. My credit was so good I could get anything, Boy was he jealous.

We had my sister and my birthday at the house. I have pictures of me pushing cake in my sister's face, plus getting all our gifts. What a day that was Eleanor, Bud, my mother, niece and nephew were there. My sister and I celebrated our birthdays on the same day because I was born on the 16th and she was born on the 18th.

Well Christmas came Ron and I went to my mothers and then we went to his mother's up in Brewton Alabama. I liked his family especially his grandmother, she was a preacher and owned her own church. She told me that she didn't care if I was green with purple spots she still loved me.

(Please order my next book that is called **I thought I found Love, back to Prison,** This books tells you of my life living with a person who used me and takes everything I had and I go back to prison.) If you like my true stories please contact me at my personal email or through the book. Mandmoutdoorsllc@gmail.com

From Behind the badge to behind bars -

Birth to 31

This is based on his life from birth to date as he lived, this is a true story. You will hear how he was raised, abused (physically, mentally and sexually), how he trained animals, followed the goal to be a Law Enforcement Officer, came out as a gay man, got accused of murder, went to prison for robbery, released on parole, and met the devil in a relationship.

I thought I found Love, back to prison -

31 to 38

I meet the devil not the person I thought I was in love with, and then was sent back to prison because I was not going to live with a demon.

Living around Millionaires and back to prison -

38 to 51

Met a millionaire in prison and lived around millionaires after I was released from prison, and back to prison once again.

Living like a Millionaire and finding my Soul mate -

51 to 59

Got out of prison, lived like a millionaire, received a Pardon from the Alabama prison system, found my soul mate but I have to wait for him to get out of prison to marry and live our life.

People that say that they cannot get ahead in life; it's because they didn't tried hard enough. I was in prison from 1986 to 1995 got out got a job and purchased a home, stayed out six years. I went back to prison because of false testimony in 2001. I stayed in prison until 2004, on release from prison I got a job and rented a trailer. I bought a house in 2009. In 2015 I was sent back to prison for defending my property and lost everything again. I stayed in prison until March 28, 2017. I got a job helping a friend. I brought my fiends business from $100.000.00 in the hole to over $12 million in 4 years. I own my home and 3 vehicles; I received a Pardon from the State of Alabama on October 26, 2023.

If you have never been incarcerated and lost everything you have in live three times and still cannot stand on your own two feet you have a problem and habit you need to get rid of. If I can get out of prison and own everything I have in less than 6 years. You can make it in life without every going to prison.

Printed in the United States
by Baker & Taylor Publisher Services